I0052103

Precision Recruitment Skills

Precision Recruitment Skills

How to Find the Right Person
For the Right Job, the First Time

Rod Matthews

BUSINESS EXPERT PRESS

Precision Recruitment Skills: How to Find the Right Person For the Right Job, the First Time
Copyright © Business Expert Press, LLC, 2018.

All rights reserved. No part of this publication may be reproduced, stored in a retrieval system, or transmitted in any form or by any means— electronic, mechanical, photocopy, recording, or any other except for brief quotations, not to exceed 250 words, without the prior permission of the publisher.

First published in 2018 by
Business Expert Press, LLC
222 East 46th Street, New York, NY 10017
www.businessexpertpress.com

ISBN-13: 978-1-94819-806-6 (paperback)
ISBN-13: 978-1-94819-807-3 (e-book)

Business Expert Press Human Resource Management and Organizational Behavior Collection

Collection ISSN: 1946-5637 (print)
Collection ISSN: 1946-5645 (electronic)

Cover and interior design by S4Carlisle Publishing Services Private Ltd., Chennai, India

First edition: 2018

10 9 8 7 6 5 4 3 2 1

Printed in the United States of America.

Dedication

For my dear Father, Charles Matthews
For my dear Mother, Dorothy Olive Matthews
(I will always miss you)

Abstract

This book is great for anyone in management who has ever experienced the stress, frustration, and costs associated with poor recruitment decisions. Presented in an easy-to-read, engaging, step-by-step format, Rod Matthews has detailed practical ways to reduce the time and money spent on recruitment, while increasing the likelihood of recruiting the right person the first time. Complete with practical exercises, it contains insightful steps for improving skills around recruitment advertising, interview preparation, interviewing candidates, and what happens after the interview. In this humorous and engaging book, Rod Matthews, the Australian facilitator and presenter often referred to as "the best trainer in Australia," offers key insights from his extensive experience in dealing with people at all levels of organizations. It is highly recommended as a must-read manual for anyone who's job involves recruitment.

Keywords

developing team, developing team members, hiring skills, hiring staff, interviewing candidates, management, recruit people, recruit staff, recruitment book, recruitment cost, recruitment process, recruitment skills

Contents

How to Get the Most Out of This Book

Rod Matthews' books are best read with a pencil in hand ready to take part in practical activities, exercises and to record your thoughts, feelings, and experiences. In order to get the most out of this book, please be prepared to participate, record, and reflect as well as read.

The aim of this book is to provide you with lots of tips, tools, and techniques that you can actually use to leverage the success of yourself and others.

There are a variety of ways you can use Rod's books:

For Self-paced Learning

The books are put together in a way that will allow you or a work colleague to complete the learning at their own pace.

To Form Part of Training Sessions or Workshops

Please feel free to copy the material in this book to form part of your training sessions or workshops. All references made to material in this book to acknowledge Rod Matthews.

As a Resource in Your Organization's Learning Centre

Combined, Rod Matthews' books form an excellent library for any business interested in investing in their workforce or for any individual interested in investing in their own education.

Disclaimer

The material in this publication is of the nature of general comment only, and neither purports nor intends to be advice. The author and publisher expressly disclaim all and any liability to any person, whether a purchaser of this publication or not, in respect of anything and of the consequences of anything done or omitted to be done by any such person in reliance, whether whole or partial, upon the whole or any part of the contents of this publication.

Acknowledgments

Most of what we know is a result of the amalgamation of personal experience, conversations with others and reading. With this in mind, it would be impossible to acknowledge every person who has truly contributed to this book.

Team members, course participants, work colleagues, friends and family have all played a role in building the book that you are holding in your hands.

There are of course some people in particular that I must mention.

Family

My wife and best friend, Margaret. Thank you for all your love, support and honesty. To my boys Liam and Riley, thank you for putting all the corporate stuff into perspective and wrestling with dad when he needed a break.

Mentor

I have had the privilege of owning a business with Robert Scanlon who has been a role model for me on many levels. A large part of this book is as much Robert as it is me.

A Special Mention

Garry King is the founder and principle of Kingscroft Consulting and has been in the recruitment industry for over 10 years. His expertise and experience have been greatly utilized in the writing of this book. Thank you Garry.

Book Reviewers

I have also had the privilege of getting to know some people through my work that I would count first and foremost as my friends. These people very kindly offered their time and considerable experience to provide me with some exceptional feedback which has greatly increased the practicality and professionalism of this book. Thank you again:

- Kylie Sprott
- Steve Mitchinson
- John Lambert
- Tracey Chapman-Marks
- Peta Bayman
- Chris Sutton

CHAPTER 1

The Cost of Getting Recruitment Wrong

The Right Person in the Right Job, First Time

I can understand that, at the beginning of a book such as this, you might be thinking a number of different things to yourself. For example, you might be thinking:

> Thanks very much but I don't have the time. If you could see the thickness of my in-tray, if you could count the number of emails that are stacking up at this very moment, if you knew the number of people who are looking for me. I don't have the time to read this book and I certainly don't have the time to recruit.

Or you might be thinking . . .

> Recruitment is not rocket science. Either they can do the job or they can't. If they can, then great, they get the job. If they can't, then fine, we find someone with a pulse who can! And you have written a whole book on this?

Or you might be thinking . . .

> Listen, I've been around a bit. I've worked for a number of different organizations in a number of different capacities and recruited more than my fair share of people in my time. So I know what it takes to find the right person. What could this book possibly hold for me that I don't already know?

No matter what you are thinking or feeling at this point, this book that you hold in your hands and have chosen to read this far, is an excellent opportunity to do a number of things.

Look at what you can do to reduce the amount of time that recruitment and interviewing take:

1. You can streamline the process so that you increase the quality of people you attract and select while minimizing the time and effort to do so.
2. This book provides you with an excellent opportunity to add to your bottom line. Recruiting with increased precision will
   - increase your profitability
   - reduce your costs
   - improve the productivity of your team.

   In some cases you will be able to multiply the effect by gaining all of these benefits.
3. The skills and ideas in this book, when implemented, will reduce the stress and frustration that can be associated with having to deal with underperforming team members. How much of your time in the past has been spent trying to improve the performance of people who seem to be square pegs in round holes?
4. You also have an excellent opportunity to look at what makes the difference between a *good* recruiter and an *excellent* recruiter.

A good recruiter might stand a better than 50-percent chance of finding a satisfactory operator who, with a little coaching and the occasional counseling, will perform to expectations.

An exceptional recruiter, a precision recruiter, will:

- not only find the right person, someone who is highly competent and highly committed
- also ensure that they have identified the right job, not just the one that has been vacated
- be able to do this with an error rate of almost nil.

Think for a moment about all the interviews and recruitment processes that you have been part of. It could have been that you were going for a job as a candidate. Or you may have been running the process. It could have been that you were one of a number of interviewers. Which of these would you rate as being good or better. Chances are there wouldn't be too many.

Now if you take away the ones that just made good, leaving you with the very good or better. Now you would be culling the list.

Now if I asked you to take out the ones that were very good, so that you are left with only the exceptional, chances are that there are very few examples you can think of. And those that do come to mind stand out clearly. You probably even thought of them first.

So this book is an excellent opportunity to identify what the precision recruiter does that the good one doesn't. And to find out how to do more precision recruitment and less of the average.

But first try this quick quiz . . .

Interviewer's Self-assessment

	Always				Never
Do you analyze job requirements in the light of business direction before beginning the recruitment process?	5	4	3	2	1
Do you seriously explore alternatives to recruiting when a position becomes vacant?	5	4	3	2	1
Do you brief and canvas the opinion of other key stakeholders in the position being recruited for?	5	4	3	2	1
Do you know how to write an effective job specification and job advertisement that will start the filtering process?	5	4	3	2	1
Do you determine Key Selection Criteria for each position and update these each time the position becomes available?	5	4	3	2	1
Do you study the qualifications of the applicant in light of the Key Selection Criteria before each interview?	5	4	3	2	1
Do you develop a unique interview plan for each position dependent on job requirements?	5	4	3	2	1
Do you begin the interview by establishing a relaxed climate conducive to open communication?	5	4	3	2	1
Do you easily build rapport with each applicant to ensure they are at ease and able to perform at their best?	5	4	3	2	1
Do you use appropriate and legal questions crafted to draw out essential information without including the desired answer?	5	4	3	2	1
Do you listen responsively more than you talk?	5	4	3	2	1

	Always				Never
Do you listen between the lines, noticing the words the candidate chooses and understanding from their words what they will be like to work with?	5	4	3	2	1
Do you easily identify the candidate's underlying values so you select the right person for your organization and team?	5	4	3	2	1
Do you adhere to employment opportunity and anti-discrimination guidelines?	5	4	3	2	1
Do you follow a planned interview format and record key points?	5	4	3	2	1
Do you know your decision-making strategies and how they can help or hinder your decisions?	5	4	3	2	1
Do you provide the applicant with information about the organization and the job? And are you able to answer their questions?	5	4	3	2	1

How Did You Score?

17–35: Ouch! You Are a Liability . . .

You are causing your team, your organization, your candidates, and your-self some serious problems. The good news is that you are best positioned to learn most from this book and when you take action on what you have learnt, you are most likely to clearly see the multiplier effect on your bot-tom line of improving your recruitment practices.

35–51: You Need Help . . .

You are taking a "bums on seats" approach to recruitment. It may result in quick replacements but as we shall see later in this chapter, you are probably costing yourself more than the speedy replacements are making for you. The good news for you is that if you implement the ideas and skills covered in this book, you will enjoy a dramatic improvement in your profitability.

52–68 Not Bad . . .!

You know what you should be doing. You just don't do it all the time. There are a number of ideas and skills in this book that can streamline your process and improve the quality of the people you get to work with.

69–85 Awesome. You Rule . . .

Please consider becoming a recruitment consultant. Not only would you clean up financially, but you would also improve the recruitment industry's standing in the corporate world from parasite to provider.

No Matter What You Scored . . .

. . . if you read this book looking for what you don't know, tracking for what is new and different, then you will undoubtedly learn something that could save you time, effort, money, *and* credibility as a manager.

Some Important Recruitment Lessons

But first, allow me to introduce myself. I left school, I guess as many people do, with no clear understanding as to what I wanted to do after school. Fortunately, in some respects, I just got enough marks to go to university. So I went for a whole year and failed abysmally. Why? Because I found it very hard to fit any study into the hectic social calendar you have to keep when living on campus.

Two days before an exam or assignment due date, I would think to myself, OK Rod, If you're going to cram an entire term's worth of work, now is the time to start! So I would set myself up: books at reachable distance, pot of coffee on the boil, and a couple of No-Doze pills had been ingested. (No-Doze pills are 100 mg of caffeine. They are evil things! I'm sure truckies take them! You can feel the hairs on the back of your neck growing after a couple of these.) Take a couple of these and you are going to stay awake for a good few hours yet!

Just as I was about to put pen to paper when there would be a knock at the door.

"Rod we're going to the pub. What are you doing?"

"Give me two minutes. I'll be with you."

There were people at university who were able to do both—kill brain cells on a nightly basis and pass with honors. I was not one of them. So I deferred after first year with the grand plan of getting a job for a year to earn enough to put myself through the rest of the degree.

I remember telling this to one of my tutors before I left. She responded with, "Well Rod, it was nice knowing you!"

I asked, "What do you mean?"

She replied, "Ninety percent of people who defer studies after their first year do not come back. So . . . it was nice knowing you, Rod!"

Obviously she had a little more experience with that than I did. And she turned out to be right. I didn't go back. Instead I found a job in a bank, and enjoyed an entry-level position that allowed me to continue with the party lifestyle and still have some money in the wallet at the end of it.

First Lesson in Recruitment

This is where I first came into contact with the concept of recruitment. Each branch of the bank had a branch manager. In those days this was a respected position held by someone with greying hair and substantial standing in the community. The branch manager would be responsible for all aspects of running the branch, including recruitment and selection.

Let's say that Jennifer is the manager of Centreville branch and her team includes a wide variety of performers. Some are great performers who have a lot of experience, love their job and take their work but not themselves seriously. Then there are the good, the average and, unfortunately, the bad. One of whom is named Graham.

Graham will never be a highflyer. The rest of the team will always need to carry him. Silly errors, short fuse, does the bare minimum. Jennifer has not dealt with Graham's performance in a constructive manner. She has been asking her good operators to fix his errors, look after poorly treated customers, and stay behind when necessary to make sure the team meets targets. Jennifer is a weak manager, it's just that she has had difficulty putting Graham's poor performance into words that won't start an hour-long debate.

You are the manager from nearby Surfside branch and you have just recently lost one of your top performers. You phone Centreville to see if they have anyone who can fill the position. Jennifer spots the opportunity and recommends Graham.

Jennifer says, "I've got a guy called Graham who is ready for that position but I'm a little reluctant to let him go as he is showing a lot of promise at the moment."

Excitedly you reply, "He sounds perfect. Now, Jennifer, you know it is bank policy that you send his file over to me to look at. That's the least you can do."

"All right," says Jennifer in mock surrender, "I'll send you Graham's file only because I have to. But I'm not promising you that I'll release him."

You are now looking at Graham's file. You have no knowledge of what he is like to work with. All you have to go on is in performance appraisals and file notes. This is not dissimilar to looking at a résumé. After reading the file you realize that Graham has the skills and experience you are looking for and after some negotiation with Jennifer she releases him. You have your position filled and Graham gets a promotion.

And we used to wonder why the bank was run by deadwood!

A skilled recruiter will be able to read between the lines of a résumé. They are able to see what is not written on a résumé. They are able to analyze the words chosen and the words that were avoided. They recognize that "years of experience" could be translated into "will be bored with this job under 6 months." "Team player" could be translated into "unable to work autonomously."

The Clone Syndrome

After working through various positions in the bank, I decided that it was time to move on. I found a job working as part of the human resources team with a well-known marketer and wholesaler of quality electronic equipment.

Part of the role was to assist managers with recruiting. We made a good team. The line managers were excellent at asking the technical questions: "So let's say that you have an SJP-1. And let's say that the timing device has failed. Describe your problem-solving process from that point on."

And the HR representative would be there to gauge what the candidate would be like to work with, their attitude and their work ethic.

There were a number of managers there who were known to suffer from the clone syndrome, that is two types of recruiting, as follows.

Someone Like Me!

This type recruits people who are most like themselves. This is because we achieve rapport when the differences between us have been minimized and the similarities maximized. It is often difficult to notice when this is happening. We just feel more comfortable with some people than others. This does not mean that they are necessarily the best person for the job.

I have seen managers recruit team members who are close to incompetent social land mines because they "seemed to get on with them," "felt comfortable with them," or even "reminded me of myself when I was younger."

Someone Like the Person Who Just Left!

This other version of "the clone syndrome" involves recruiting someone who is most like the person who just left. "Sally's gone. We need another Sally."

If the person was an exceptional performer, this might be fine. What a precision recruiter would do, however, is check that those skills and attitudes are still relevant, that the position has not changed and that advances have not been made in the technology that surrounds the job. Recruiting someone like the person who just left can easily lead to stagnation . . . which leads neatly into the next point.

How the Professionals Do It

I also worked with a number of recruitment consultancies. I know that recruitment consultants are not thought of too well in corporate circles . . . and rightfully so in many cases. The recruitment consultancy is largely a sales organization with a sales culture and a *bums on seats* mentality. It's the plumber's house where the taps leak. It's the mechanic's car that needs a tune up. It's the recruitment consultancy that needs to improve the quality of its culture and people.

There are, however, many very good recruiters out there. They will take a brief and ask you questions such as:

- What is the position responsible for?
- What did you most like/dislike about the previous incumbent?
- What are you looking for in the successful candidate?

These are all relevant questions, but most of them concern the job at hand and the current situation.

A precision recruiter will want to know about the bigger picture and the near future so their questions will more likely be:

- What is it like working here?
- How would you describe the culture of the organization?
- What does the organization value?
- Why do you need to recruit?
- What is your organization's direction over the next 2 to 3 years?
- How will that affect your department/division?
- What are the implications for this particular role?

Paying for Recruitment Errors

Let's build a list of all the costs associated with losing one employee and then replacing them with another.

In order to help us generate an accurate list of the true costs, we can think about two types of costs on five different levels.

The two types of costs are:

1. **Direct costs:** These are the easy ones. They are the most obvious and have a dollar amount attached to them. Examples are advertising, consultants etc.
2. **Indirect costs:** These are a little harder to identify. They are often not measured, are difficult to quantify, and there is rarely a dollar amount. Examples are manager's time, error rates, etc.

And these costs can be found at five different levels, that is:

A) to customers
B) to the organization
C) to the team, department, or division
D) to the candidate
E) to you—the manager

In no particular order and without grouping them into the above categories, here is an extensive, but not exhaustive, list of costs associated with poor recruitment:

- recruitment consultants
- advertising
- temporary staff fees
- salary paid to the candidate who didn't work out
- potential loss of customers
- potential loss of business
- errors made by the team member who didn't work out
- errors made by new team member coming up to speed
- work not completed while replacement is being found
- candidate's self esteem
- candidate's view of your company passed on to other people in the industry
- damage to your reputation as a manager
- extra effort from your team to carry the workload
- potential legal fees from unfair dismissal
- your time coaching the new team member
- your team members' time coaching the new team member
- formal training costs
- on costs like superannuation, workers compensation, payroll tax etc.
- consumables, stationary, and equipment
- your time dealing with the person who left
- your time dealing with the person who didn't work out
- your time working with human resources to determine how to resolve the situation
- Human Resources' time working with you to determine how to resolve the situation
- your managers' time being kept up to date of events
- your organization's profile in an incestuous industry
- your profile as a manager in an incestuous industry

People who make a study of human resources in organizations have crunched the numbers and determined that the cost of losing a team member and replacing them with a new team member is on average two and a half times the salary of the position. There are also those in the industry that would say two and half times the person's salary is a conservative figure!!!

Two and a half times the salary of the position! Can you believe it? It is hard to believe at first, I'll admit, but when you look at the list of costs above and you add some that are specific to your situation, it starts to become conservative.

Do some maths for me . . . , for yourself!

How many people left your team in the last 12 months?   _____(N)
What was the average salary of the people who left?   _____(S)

So to calculate how much money you lost due to turnover last year:

$$N \times S \times 2.5 =$$

For example:

How many people left your team in the last 12 months?   9_____(N)
What was the average salary of the people who left? $45,000 (S)

This means that turnover last year cost us:

$$9 \times \$45,000 \times 2.5 = \$1,012,500.00$$

How would that look as increased profit? Tasty? Then read on . . .

Now I'm not advocating that no turnover is ideal. Nil turnover can lead to stagnation. I once consulted to one of the early organizations in the IT industry. They wrote programs in one of the first computer languages used. Many other organizations were keen to make use of this amazingly efficient technology at the time and so bought in to this language, boots, and all. As a result, many of them still use this language as a basis for their programs even though the language is now quite ancient in IT terms.

To maintain a service to its client base in the language, the organization that created the program had to retain its employees as much as possible because new people entering the IT industry did not want to use the language. The average length of service in the organization was 23 years.

The organization was crippled. It was in a declining market with long-term loyal team members who were being paid very senior salaries, funded by increasingly shrinking contracts.

The same types of people who crunched the numbers to determine that turnover is equivalent to two and a half times an employee's salary also determined that a healthy turnover rate is around the 10 percent mark. That is, every 12 months it is useful for the growth of your business that 10 percent of your team leave and are replaced by new blood.

Alternatives to Recruitment

There are, of course, alternatives to recruiting. If you want to assist the growth of your business, remain competitive, learn new ways of doing things, redistribute budgets, and save costs; it would be wise to seriously consider these alternatives.

Below is an extensive, yet not exhaustive, list of questions to prompt your thinking on alternatives to recruitment. As you read these questions some obvious answers will jump to mind. Try to suspend your final judgment until you have considered both the benefits and the drawbacks of each suggestion.

What would happen if:

- we promoted from within?
- the role was completed by a part timer?
- the person was not replaced by anyone?
- the role was divided among the remaining team members?
- we automated the positions with technology?
- we restructured the organization?
- we outsourced the tasks to another organization?
- we asked a contractor to complete the tasks?
- we stopped offering those products/services to our clients?
- we asked our clients to take responsibility for those tasks?
- we asked another department/division to complete those tasks?

Best Practice Recruitment

Having considered the alternatives, in most cases you will still need to recruit. So now the question becomes, What do I need to do?

After having spent a number of years in and around recruitment, the team at Impact decided to identify a Best Practice Recruitment process.

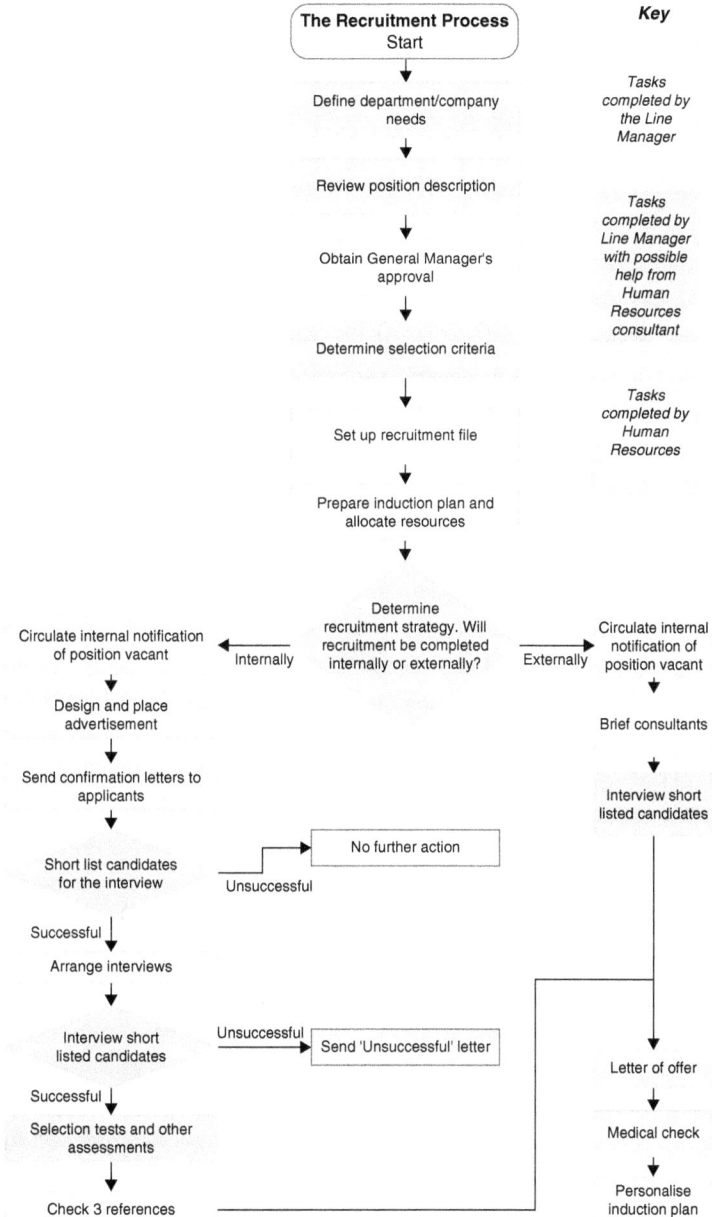

To do this we called on the experience and expertise of a number of leading organizations that were not only known as setting the standard in recruitment, but also had enough resources in the organization to have individuals, sometimes whole teams, whose role it was to purely manage the recruitment of their organization.

As a result of this research, we designed the process you see below. Please keep in mind that this process will vary for you depending on:

- how much human resource support your company offers
- whether your organization is public or private
- whether your company has any alliances with recruitment providers.

Pick Any Two . . .

As mentioned earlier, I used to work for a well-known marketer and wholesaler of quality electronic equipment. Among other things, they sold TVs. There was a service section where our in-house technicians would work on products that the company's independent service technicians had been unable to fix.

As you walked into the service section from outside, you would see a sign above the service counter that read:

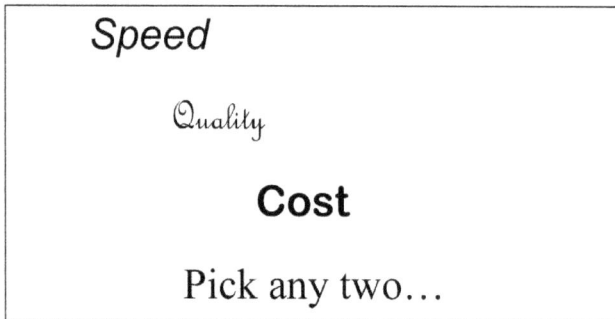

> *Speed*
>
> *Quality*
>
> **Cost**
>
> Pick any two...

The sign implies a number of things:

- If you want your TV fixed and you want it done quickly and well, then we will charge you. We will charge you because we will need to take other people off other jobs and get them to focus on yours.

> As well as that we will also need to use top quality components and all of that costs money.
> - If you want your TV fixed and you want it done quickly and cheaply, that's fine but we will not guarantee the quality.
> - If you want your TV fixed and you want a good quality job done at a bargain basement price, then we will take our time.

On the one hand, this could be limiting belief. Perhaps it is possible to have all three. Yet research shows that often companies fail because they are trying to be all things to all people. The companies that thrive and survive are those that have found their niche and stuck to it.

That is why in most advertising you will see either overtly or covertly stated that the company claims to offer one or two of those things.

Speed   "When it absolutely has to be there overnight." "Convenience." "You can spend more time doing what is important to you."

Quality   "When only the best will do." "Guaranteed." "Notice the difference."

Cost   "We will match/beat any quote." "The cheapest in town." "At these prices they won't last."

The same is true for you at work on a number of levels:

- On a macro level
- Managing yourself
- As a precision recruiter

On a Macro Level

As a manager you are responsible for the output of your team. It is wise to think about in what niche your team needs to play in order to be the best it can be for your organization, your customers, and your team members.

Is your team the team that always meets its deadlines? If something urgent needs to be done, do you send in your team?

Is yours the team that gets it right every time? The team that dots the Is and crosses the Ts? And the team that produces a level of product or service that others only aspire to?

Is your team the most economic? The team that always does more with less? No matter what the budget, no matter what the equipment, no matter what the support, will your team be able to do something?

Managing Yourself

On a daily basis you have to decide what you are going to do at the expense of what you are not going to get done. At work and in life there are unlimited things to do in a limited time frame. So you need to make decisions about how you spend your time.

"Speed, quality, cost. Pick any two . . ." is an excellent tool to help you make these decisions. Every time a task lands on your desk, every time someone asks you to do something, every time you look at your To Do List, ask yourself, What is the priority order for this task? Speed, quality, or cost?

That is not to say that you will not try for all three. Of course you will. You are a good manager, a good team member, a good corporate citizen. I'm not asking you, What are you going to sacrifice? I'm asking you, What is the priority order for this task?

As a Precision Recruiter

The same is true for recruitment. As you were looking at the precision recruitment process, you may have found yourself thinking, You want me to do what? How long does all that take? I don't have time for all that.

That's fine. I understand that there are many things competing for your time. All I'm pointing out is that the "Speed, quality, cost. Pick any two . . ." dynamic holds true for recruitment as well.

Sure you can cut corners if you want and if you do, there will be one of two consequences. Either you will be recruiting someone who is inappropriate and you will be trying to manage them out within 12 months or you will be paying big bucks to a consultant to do the recruitment for you.

The choice is yours. Make it a conscious choice.

CHAPTER 2

Precision Recruitment Process

Triggers to Recruit

It is easy to fall into the trap of having only one trigger to highlight the need for you to recruit. Someone leaves so we need to recruit. This can be another one-way ticket to stagnation. Managers who wait for someone to leave before they recruit, or who only recruit when someone is leaving, are showing a very limited understanding of how a business works and how to grow a business. They are managing by reaction rather than managing proactively.

There could be several reasons why a savvy manager might consider it was appropriate to recruit:

- The organization's strategic plan calls for a growth phase.
- The market in which you operate is expanding.
- Your business has diversified.
- Your business has consolidated.
- Your organization is restructuring.
- Team members are stressed out.
- Turnover is high.
- Sick leave is high.
- Error rates are high.
- Deadlines are being missed.
- Your organization has won a large contract/new piece of work.
- Mergers and acquisitions have occurred.
- Assistance is required with succession planning.
- Employee has announced pregnancy.

- Employee is due to retire.
- Corporate rumor has arisen that there will soon be a headcount freeze.

And, of course, really savvy managers are always on the lookout for good people, working on the idea that the right people will build the business for you.

How to Avoid the "Clone Syndrome"

As you may remember from Chapter 1 of this book, the Clone Syndrome has two types:

1. **Someone like me!**
   People recruit someone most like themselves.
2. **Someone like the person who just left!**
   People recruit someone most like the person who just left.

Either way we need to be sure that we are not falling into the same trap. A precision recruiter does several things to reduce the chances of the candidate being a clone.

The first thing is to clearly define the organization's needs by doing a simple gap analysis.

Your Mission—Gap Analysis

Congratulations! You have just been selected to join the army and you are currently in a briefing room at the RAAF base. The Squadron Leader is briefing you:

Good morning, troops! Today at precisely 0800 hours you will take part in your first test mission. You will board one of our Hercules aircraft with complete kit and parachute. You will be flown to an undisclosed location where you will parachute out of the aircraft. Upon landing you will be allowed access to the four envelopes, each of which contains different information about components of your mission. You must only open three of the four envelopes. Using the information you have access to, you must find your way to the rendezvous point before 1800 hours when transport will arrive to bring you back to base. Any questions . . .? Jolly good. Best of luck.

At precisely 0800 you find yourself boarding an RAAF Hercules aircraft. If you have ever been on one of these you will know that the trap is not quite first class. You sit on a mesh seat with one or two other people. It is so noisy inside that it is hard to talk and the cabin service is probably tactfully described as nonexistent. The plane takes off, then circles, dips, and banks so all sense of direction is lost. After what seems like hours of flying, the signal is given. Your parachute is hooked up to a line and when there is no one in front of you, it's your turn to jump.

After landing, as discussed, you examine the four envelopes and remember that you are only allowed to use three to get you to the rendezvous point. The envelopes are labelled as shown here. As you read the labels, consider for a moment which envelope is least important to you.

Most people recognize almost instantly that Envelope 1 is unlikely to contain any information that will help us complete our mission. The key envelopes, in no specific order, are:

- Your current location
- The path to the rendezvous point
- The rendezvous point

This seems logical enough in this context. And yet in business many people make decisions using only the information from envelope one, what has happened in the past. This is also true of many managers who are recruiting.

To be a precision recruiter you will need to use the information from Envelopes 2, 3, and 4, as follows. This is otherwise called simple gap analysis.

First, build an understanding of where the organization, your department or team and, therefore, the position you are recruiting for will be in the future.

Then contrast that with where the organization, your department, or team is now and therefore where the position you are recruiting for is now.

And also consider what the path along the way will hold for the organization, your department, or team and the position you are recruiting for.

The Michael Parkinson Interview

Think of a position that you are likely to be recruiting for in the not-too-distant future. It could be one that is vacant as you are reading this book, it could be a common position at your work, it could be one that experiences regular turnover.

Use this position as an example to work on as you read through the book. That way when the time comes to recruit for that position, you will have done your planning and be ready to go.

To help you do the gap analysis with your own example position, imagine that you are the special guest star on The Michael Parkinson Show. You might know of Michael Parkinson. He has been interviewing famous people for many years. He seems to have an amazing ability to tease out things from his guests that few other interviewers could.

As you enter the set, the TV audience is on an ad break, Michael welcomes you and you take a seat next to him. The camera focuses on Michael and the producer counts us back to live broadcasting. "Three . . . two and . . ."

As the producer points to Michael, the red light on the camera comes on and Michael says, "Thanks very much for coming back. My next guest is a manager in an organization in the throes of recruiting for a certain position and, as such, they are in an excellent situation to give us an insight into where the organization is headed and what that means for the successful applicant."

Michael turns to you and officially welcomes you to the show, to which you respond with, "It's a pleasure to be here, Michael," Michael then asks you the following questions.

(Please note your answers in the space provided)

Michael asks, "What would you say is the most desirable situation possible for:

- your organization?
- your department/team?
- the position you are advertising?"

You cleverly answer:

Michael says, "Some excellent distinctions there. That obviously reflects a considerable understanding of the market's direction. But how does that differ from the current situation:

- of your organization?
- of your department/team?
- of the position you are advertising?"

You weave your magic once again by saying:

Michael, now almost lost for words with your brilliance, says, "Well I think that we would all agree that there are some amazingly insightful observations in what you say. Tell us what potential challenges would it be wise to plan for as you move from the current situation to the desired situation:

- for your organization?
- for your department/team?
- for the position?"

And now stupefied audience hangs on the edge of their seat as you tell them:

As Michael breaks his astonished glare to wipe the dribble from the corner of his mouth, he thanks you most sincerely for your time and insights and turns back to the camera now focused on him to lead the audience back to an ad break. (All right, maybe the dribble was going a little too far. No matter.)

Think for a moment about the benefit of answering these questions and thinking about the business in this fashion.

Most average managers don't do this. Ever! They are promoted from the ranks of team member into a position of management and are still thinking like a team member. Team members are often focused on the past. You can hear it in the words they use:

- "This is how we have done it in the past."
- "That didn't work last time we tried it."
- "In my experience . . ."

This is useful, and in some cases necessary, when you were a team member who was employed because of your past experience.

The difficulty arises when the team member tries to talk to an entrepreneurial CEO. The CEO will have future-based language:

- "This is where we are headed."
- "The market is leading us to . . ."
- "By the end of next period . . ."

and the particularly popular and extremely useless

- ". . . moving forward . . ."

Part of your role as an exceptional manager is to act as a translator. To take the corporate strategic plan, the corporate intent, the mission, the vision, the values, the whatever, and translate it into a language that your team members not only can understand but are enthusiastic to be a part of.

So the benefit of answering these questions is that you have started to think more as your boss thinks and more like a manager. Now you will be able to make decisions that are more likely to benefit the business—recruitment decisions included.

Recruit for the Journey

Recruiting for Your Current Situation

If you recruit a team member to meet your current needs, they will be quick to start contributing and quick to become a liability. As I've mentioned before, recruiting someone with only the current situation in mind can lead to stagnation. Managers who recruit this way will find it difficult to implement any changes required. They will be constantly spending time and money training and coaching team members to do their job and they will be dealing with poor performance more often.

Recruiting for Your Desired Situation

Recruiting with the desired situation in mind also has its drawbacks. Candidates are lured to a job on the promise that the things they will be doing are at a certain stage. They accept the role based on the idea that the organization has evolved to a certain stage. If the organization does not make some giant steps forward within the first few months of their employment, this could lead to a big mismatch in expectations. Managers who recruit with the desired situation in mind experience high turnover within 12 months of hiring the new team member. They are constantly having to hold team members back, limit their autonomy, and micromanage them.

Recruiting for the Journey

The answer is to recruit for the journey. Look for a candidate that best matches the needs of the organization, team, and position over the next two years. Managers who recruit team members with the journey ahead in mind find that their new team members evolve with the position, the team, and the organization. They will develop themselves and the position into what the organization needs. There is an increased likelihood of a satisfied employee and that translates into a higher quality of output and an organization that is built to last.

Key Selection Criteria

My wife Margaret and I have a shopping problem. Margaret will spend $5 buying something worth $10 that we don't need. I, on the other hand, will spend $10 on something worth $5 that we do need.

Margaret could compete for Australia in the Bargain Hunter Olympics and would benefit from only going to the shops when she has something that we need to buy in mind, heading straight for that item and ignoring all other distractions on the way.

I shop with purpose. I'm only there when I know exactly what I want. So I march into the store, go straight to the item I need, don't even look at the price, get to the cash register, and as I reach into my wallet I think to myself, "That's a little on the expensive side, isn't it?" I would benefit from setting myself a maximum price that I should pay and then being prepared to spend a little more time comparing prices.

If we could combine our shopping talents I'm sure we would have enough money left over to feed the kids!

When it comes to recruitment, a precision recruiter will combine these talents. They recognize that you must be clear about what they are looking for before they "go to the shops." They also recognize that they will need to allow a little time to explore, consider, and compare.

The way to do this in recruiting is to be clear about your Key Selection Criteria. What is it that the candidate must have, be, or do before you are prepared to work with them?

Key Selection Criteria are usually general statements of skill, experience, ethics, and values. Where do they come from? From the answers to your Michael Parkinson interview questions and from your analysis of what is required in the position for the journey to the desired situation. Revisit your answers in the earlier part of this chapter and see if you can identify five key things that your next team member must have, do, or be.

Some examples include:

- Superior customer-service skills
- Advanced communication skills
- Proven problem-solving ability
- Ability to meet deadlines
- Initiative
- Ability to follow procedures
- Resourcefulness and awareness of a need for economy
- Attention to detail
- Ability to build rapport with a wide range of people
- Strong track record in sales
- Solid product knowledge
- Comprehensive industry experience
- Strong work ethic
- Ability to work autonomously
- Ability to work as part of a team
- Well-developed decision-making ability
- Technical skill to level 5

Try and stick to five Key Selection Criteria only. Any more than that, and you are probably trying to find superman or you are being too specific. Any less than that, and the position is not a serious position or you are being too general.

If you have tried your best and you still have more than five Key Selection Criteria, use the "must/should/could" method of focusing on what you are looking for in the position.

- **Must have**—without these skills or abilities the candidate will not make it to the next stage in the recruitment process.
- **Should have**—these are skills or abilities the candidate should have, although they are negotiable yet desirable.
- **Could have**—these are a bonus. By the same token, if the candidate does not have these qualities, they may still be successful.

Think about your own example position you will be recruiting for in the future and record what you would consider to be the five Key Selection Criteria for that position.

Key Selection Criteria 1:

Key Selection Criteria 2:

Key Selection Criteria 3:

Key Selection Criteria 4:

Key Selection Criteria 5:

If you ever read the job advertisements in the newspapers or on the Internet, you can easily see what the Key Selection Criteria for the position will be.

How to Obtain Approval

Have you ever seen the BBC series "Yes, Minister" or "Yes, Prime Minister"? These are comedy series about the Westminster system of government and how it works. While the characters and setting are certainly very British, the situations could as easily be played out in Australian government or indeed most democracies.

There are three central characters:

- the likeable, yet mostly ineffectual, minister who, in the later series, becomes prime minister.

- the career civil servant, Sir Humphrey Appleby, through whom the series writers suggests (convincingly so) that the civil service actually runs the country more than the politicians.
- the minister's secretary, Bernard, who is relatively new to all the political games that are being played and asks the questions we, the audience, often want to ask.

In one of the episodes, Sir Humphrey needs to have the minister decide on a course of action with the minister believing that it was his decision and not Sir Humphrey's. Bernard asks how Sir Humphrey will be certain that the minister will select the course of action Sir Humphrey wants.

Sir Humphrey replies to Bernard that there are five words you can include in any proposed course of action that will guarantee that the minister will not select that suggestion. Those words are:

- difficult
- expensive
- unpopular
- inconclusive
- uncertain.

And to be more than 100 percent certain that a minister will not select a course of action you should include the words "electorally brave."

Equally, Sir Humphrey suggests there are five words that will guarantee that the minister *will* select a certain course of action. These words are:

- easy
- economic
- popular
- definite
- proven.

Now, while I'm not suggesting that the field of persuasion and influence is as simple as the inclusion or exclusion of five words, the idea of carefully choosing the language you use when you wish to be persuasive is a useful one.

Unless you know that the recruitment will be approved as a matter of course, you will need to do a bit of homework before obtaining approval from the powers that be in your organization.

There will be a language that the decision makers will need to hear in order for them to justify their approval. Remember that these people are often the ones in the organization who sign the checks or are responsible for budgets and have to answer to boards or shareholders.

Notice the difference between the following examples.

Line-manager language	Decision-maker language
I've lost one of my best operators. I need your approval to replace them before I go crazy and my team rebels.	Colleen, the team member who saved us hundreds of thousands of dollars last year, has left and the sooner I can replace her the less money we will lose.
I need to recruit a replacement for Colleen.	Reaching the targets we set earlier this year will have to be put on hold until we can find a replacement for Colleen.
Look, I know that we are trying to keep costs down at the moment but I really need to replace Colleen. So could I please have your approval to begin recruitment?	I was thinking last night about the costs of having Colleen's old position left vacant. As well as the potential loss of revenue, there is also likely to be an increase in the error rate as we try to spread the workload and a potential blow out of the budget as we scramble to fix errors without loss on customers.

The key here is to link it into WIIFM—What's In It For Me! In this case, "Me" is the person whose approval you need.

CHAPTER 3

Advertising and Dealing with the Response

Finding the Right Person

What Are Your Options?

At this stage in the recruitment process there are a number of options available to you. These include:

- using a consultant
- to search or to advertise?
- doing it yourself
- looking within the organization
- looking outside the organization
- advertising in the print media
- advertising on the Internet.

Let's explore each of these options.

Using a Consultant

I can understand that to some people using a consultant is about as attractive as using cold-sore cream. Consultants are often ranked just above used-car salespeople and politicians on the food chain. This is not totally without reason. There are some rotten consultants out there, little better than charlatan status. But there are some exceptional recruitment and search consultants as well.

Finding a good consultant is not unlike finding a good team member. It will require similar skills. You will need to be clear about what you want them to do. You will want them to know where to find good candidates, interview potential candidates, listen between the lines, and do reference checks. So if you are outsourcing the role of recruitment mainly because you believe you do not have the skills internally . . . be afraid . . ., be very afraid!

There are, of course, other considerations as to why you would use a consultant:

- Is there sufficient expertise in your organization to find the specific person for this specific job?
- Are there sufficient resources (time, money, support, equipment, knowledge) in the organization to complete the entire recruitment process?
- How specialized/senior is the position?

To Search or to Advertise?

While there are exceptions to the rule, generally speaking advertising works best:

- when you are recruiting a high volume of staff.
- when the skills you are looking for could come from a variety of industries.

So if you are looking to recruit for a highly specialized position with tight criteria, searching allows access to highly specific databases, highly specific networks that your advertising might not reach.

Doing It Yourself

Have you ever worked for a manager who:

- didn't understand enough about what you do to allow you to do it well?
- was unable to get on with people who were different to themselves?
- didn't exhibit an ability to plan and prepare?
- didn't exhibit an ability to listen?
- was poor at making decisions?

Then I would strongly recommend that you don't become that manager.

Recruiting team members requires you to practice all the above skills. They are all skills that are critical for a manager at any level in any organization. Repetition is the mother of learning. Outsourcing all or even most of your recruitment means that you are losing a key, high-profile, and easily measurable opportunity to practice and display these key management skills.

I would recommend that you be closely involved with most of the recruitment process for most positions that report to you.

Looking Within the Organization and/or Looking Outside the Organization

Actions speak louder than words. In the blank space in the following table, specify all the messages you would be sending to your team members if you look within the organization or outside the organization to find your new team member.

As you do this, avoid the simple trite answers that lead you to one or the other conclusion. It is not as simple as doing one or the other or even both. It is about considering the effect before making the decision.

Messages you will send others in your organization if you look to promote someone within your organization	Messages you will send others in your organization if you look to find someone from outside your organization

Sometimes you might want to send a message to your team members that the organization is undergoing transformational change, other times it is about transactional change and sometimes it is "steady as she goes."

A poor manager will look to fill vacancies from the same pool of people every time.

It is also about more than just what message you wish to send to your organization. You also need to consider where the skill set you are looking to find exists. Sometimes the skill set requires a good working knowledge of the organization, its culture, and its customers. At other times the skill set will not exist within the organization.

The answer here is to reexamine your Key Selection Criteria and make the decision after having considered these issues, rather than responding the same way every time.

Advertising in the Print Media and/or on the Internet

Here again, it is easy to fall into rote responses: "But we always advertise in the paper." One way of working out where to advertise is to look in the different media for similar positions to the one you are looking to fill.

Check your assumptions before you place the advertisement. It is not as simple as advertising IT jobs on the Internet and Finance jobs in the *Australian Financial Review.* Most media organizations keep very detailed statistics on their readership and they are happy to provide potential advertisers with an overview.

The key question to keep in mind is, where do people with the skill set I'm looking for look for jobs?

Building an Advertisement

Increasing the Quantity of Responses

Imagine that you are looking for a job. Have a look at the two advertisements below and notice what you are thinking and feeling as you read them.

Opposition Leader Wanted	Top Quality Leader
The federal opposition is looking to replace its leadership with someone new. We are looking for a person who has had some degree of experience in politics either in the public or private arenas, with at least five years' experience in a senior position attached to an organization commercial or noncommercial in nature. The salary is in the eighty thousand to one hundred and twenty thousand a year range and while there is no room for promotion, many business supporters operate on an "if you can keep it quiet, you can keep it" basis. This will increase the salary to five hundred thousand a year. The successful applicant will be a member of the community of good standing and female as we are committed to meeting our commitment of percentage of equal opportunity. As well as shaking hands and kissing babies the successful applicant will be required to unite the party and lead then to a successful election. If you are interested please send your résumé to the attention of William Rosenkrantz, Party Whip, PO Box 0000 in your capital city. Must be practiced at making three second statements that the press cannot edit into anything other than what you meant to say.	• **Highly attractive salary package** • **High-profile position** • **Equal Opportunity employer** The federal opposition is looking to create a new direction in government. We are looking for an active, committed and responsible leader who is both intelligent and street wise. To be the successful candidate you will: • have 5 years' experience in a political arena. • be a high-profile member of the community of good standing. • exhibit advanced interpersonal and communication skills. If you are interested please send your résumé to: William Rosenkrantz Party Whip PO Box 0000 In your capital city Or you can phone William on 02 1234 5678

OK, so I had a little fun and made it obvious. Nonetheless, I have seen advertisements in the paper not too dissimilar to the one on the left. As well as the obvious language and flow, there are three key things that make the two advertisements so different.

Layout

Use the same theory as newspapers and magazines. To help attract and keep someone's attention use a variety of font sizes. Start with the biggest and then gradually shrink the fonts until you are at the details level. This will entice the reader down or filter them out, dependent on the first few lines.

Less is More

Remember to use bullet points, white space and be artfully vague (?)

Key Selection Criteria Stated

Overtly or covertly. Highlight what will be most attractive to the person you want to interview.

Increasing the Quality of Responses

Have you ever found yourself talking to someone and, although you are both speaking English, it's as if you are speaking a different language? That's because there are many sublanguages that we use that reveal our preferences. These include:

- what we prefer to focus on
- how we prefer to take in information
- how we prefer to process that information
- how we prefer to store the information
- how we prefer to re-present that information.

There are literally dozens of these preferences. If you have ever completed a personality, behavioral, or values-based profiling instrument such as DiSC, Myers Briggs (MBTI), or Team Management Index (TMI), what they do is to measure different preferences and then draw conclusions as to the benefits and drawbacks of those preferences.

Let's examine some of these preferences and think about how it would help us begin the filtering process.

Let's say that a good friend of yours has just returned from a holiday trip away. When you first see them you ask, "How was your holiday?" Depending on their preference, they will respond to this question in a number of ways.

People Preference

Some people have a preference for other people. So they might respond by saying:

> It was great. We met this lovely couple at dinner one night and . . . then we happened to see them again on a tour the next day . . . have you ever met the Fijian people? They are so friendly.

Things Preference

Some people have a preference for things. So they might respond in this way:

> It was great. I bought you this thing. See you turn it upside down and shake it and it snows on Uluru.

These people often love to shop on holidays or surround themselves with the latest and greatest. A very good friend of mine is a things person and he is always buying the latest electrical gadget whether he needs it or not. You walk into the spare room at his place and you are surrounded by computers, scanners, personal organizers, printers, etc.

Information Preference

Some people have a preference for information. So they might respond like this:

> It was great. Did you know that they have been putting people on that island since 1847. The first ship to go there actually had the same name as the first Governor who was very good at working with the locals and learning their language . . .

Never go to a slide night at my parents place. They are information people and they disagree on tiny details. So imagine sitting in a dark room looking at slide number 376 and then the following conversation starts:

> *Dad:* 'This is when we were just about to leave the south island . . .'
>
> *Mum:* 'No it's not, Hun. Don't you remember that we hadn't yet been to the cable car at this stage and we went to the cable car before we left the south island.'
>
> *Dad:* 'No. We had a cup of coffee at the cable car and you mentioned that it was just like the coffee we had in that little place in the north island.'
>
> *Mum:* 'All right! I'll go and get the travel diary . . .'
>
> *Rod thinks to himself:* 'No Mum. Don't get the travel diary. Please don't get the travel diary.'

I do love them! Really!

Place Preference

Some people have a preference for place. So they might respond by describing the places they went:

> It was great. We walked to the top of the tallest mountain and the view was just spectacular. You could see the whole city laid out before you . . . later we went to a restaurant. It was the cutest place. You walked in and the whole place was done up like something out of a 1940s musical and down one of the walls was all these hats . . .

Activity Preference

Some people have a preference for activity. So they might respond by saying this:

> "It was great. I went rock climbing, abseiling, paraflying, . . ." Or, "I did nothing! I laid out on my banana lounge, read my book and sipped slowly on the cocktails they kept serving me."

Talking about doing nothing is still talking about activity.

Careful with the Judgments

Please don't think that just because you identified with one of the above descriptions more than the others that you are "that type."

Obviously you will have an ability to notice and talk about all of those things. Also, this is all context-driven. Because I asked about a holiday, it may have skewed your response one way. If I asked "How is life outside of work?" I might get a different preference.

Occupation Preference

This preference, along with many other preferences, can be seen in career/job selection. Let's have a think about what type of jobs people with the various preferences might be drawn toward:

- People:
    - Sales
    - Service
    - Counseling/psychology
    - Hospitality
    - Beauty/Hairdressing
- Things:
    - Computers
    - Engineering
    - Mechanic
    - Spare parts
    - Building/Construction
- Information:
    - Information technology
    - Marketing
    - Librarian
    - Actuaries
    - Research

- Place:
  - Hospitality
  - Airlines
  - Travel Agency
  - Tour operators
  - Jobs at landmarks
  - Overseas assignments
- Activity:
  - Production
  - Machine operator
  - Project manager
  - Armed forces
  - Emergency services—fire, police, ambulance

Applying This to Your Advertisement

Think about your own example job that you will be recruiting for soon. Think about what preference would best suit that position.

Once you have done that, it is now a matter of matching the language that the candidate with that preference would best understand and relate to. Use phrases like these to attract people with a particular preference:

- People preference
  - You will be reporting to . . .
  - Working with a team of . . .
  - . . . large group of like-minded . . .
  - . . . family-style company . . .
  - . . . customers . . .
  - . . . liaise with . . .
- Things preference
  - . . . leading-edge equipment . . .
  - Responsible for the following materials...
  - You will be supplied with the latest laptop, mobile phone, and company car
  - Responsible for the movement and distribution of . . .
  - . . . up-to-date technology . . .
  - . . . asset management . . .

- Information preference
  - ... gathering, storage, and retrieval of information
  - ... extensive database ...
  - ... demographics ...
  - ... record, catalogue, and list ...
  - ... analysis and identification ...
- Place preference
  - ... right in the heart of the CBD
  - ... a short easy walk to ...
  - ... relaxed and informal ...
  - Work from home
  - Close to ...
  - Parking included
- Activity preference
  - Projects to be completed ...
  - Tasks include ...
  - ... the processes and procedures ...
  - ... quick response ...
  - ... activities include ...

If You Want to Attract the Best People—Start Here!

OK. So far we have looked at the following topics:

- Becoming aware of the clone syndrome and how to avoid it
- Identifying all the money we are going to save because we are recruiting with precision
- Considering alternatives to recruitment
- Identifying a best practice process
- Recognizing that as we recruit we need to determine our priority—speed, quality, cost
- Becoming aware that a smart manager will have many triggers to recruiting
- Resetting our understanding of the job we are looking to fill by doing a gap analysis
- Being on TV with Michael Parkinson

- Deciding that it is best to recruit for the journey rather than the current or desired position
- Using the distinctions gained from the Michael Parkinson interview to develop Key Selection Criteria
- Identifying some words that might help us gain approval to recruit
- Building an advertisement that will entice the reader down to the details of the job
- Building an advertisement that will speak most clearly to a person with a preference that will be useful.

Now the résumés, emails, and phone calls will start.

First Impressions—Yours and Theirs

A Word of Caution . . .!

Please note: This is quite likely to be your best candidate's first contact with your organization. If you want to attract the right person—so start here! The right person in many cases will be someone who is observant, able to draw conclusions, and has a degree of initiative. If this is the case, then a precision recruiter will go to great lengths to ensure that all contact with the candidates send the right message about what it is like to work with you.

A candidate who is observant will notice the poorly answered telephone call, the call being transferred to the wrong person, the call being transferred without introduction, the "I'm busy" or the "this is the twentieth time I've been asked this today" sound in your voice. A candidate might draw the conclusion that you lack patience, that the customer receives poor service or that working in your organization will be very stressful and unenjoyable.

A candidate who has a degree of initiative could decide that this is not the right job for them, so they will look elsewhere. Well done. You have just lost the best person for the job!

So here is an extensive, but not exhaustive, list of what can be done to create the best possible first impression. Note that if you are using an external consultant to assist with the recruiting, some of the items listed may be their responsibility.

- Be prepared. Determine a process for dealing with responses via phone, email, letter, and even face to face. Make sure that the process is as uniform as possible to increase the likelihood that all candidates have the same opportunity.
- Schedule time in your diary to field the responses to the advertisement.
- Prepare everyone for the possibility that their next team member could be contacting them today via phone. This includes the receptionist!
- Communicate the process and the job to others in your department.
- Let reception know where to transfer any phone calls.
- Determine who else can take the calls if you are busy.
- Prepare your response for phone and email.
- Prepare a standard email response to send people who have emailed their application to you.
- Answer each phone call and each question as if it was the first time you have answered that today.
- Stick to the process. Avoid telling one candidate something and another candidate something else.
- Don't overpromise or provide false expectations.
- Prepare for questions you'll be asked. For example:
  ○ What is the salary?
  ○ What are the main things you are looking for?
  ○ What is the next step?
  ○ When can we book in an interview?
  ○ How much interest have you had so far?
  Most of the time people know the answers to many of the questions they ask, they are just trying to get noticed and increase their chances of being selected.
- Advise candidates of the recruitment process—the next steps.

More Résumés in Less Time

Have you ever had the experience of buying a car? You decide on a certain make and certain model and you are driving it around for the first couple of weeks and all of a sudden you start noticing all the other cars on the road that are the same model.

Before you decided to buy that model you barely saw one, but now it seems as though the vast majority of car owners traded in their car at the same time for one like the one you have just bought.

This is obviously not the case. Vast numbers of people have not bought the same car as you at the same time as you. What has happened is that you have begun to track for that car.

There is a function of the brain called the *reticular activating system* (RAS). What the RAS does is it filters out the information that we do not need/choose to focus on and allows through the information that we need or choose.

For example, until I mention it, you are probably not consciously aware of sounds outside of the room you are in . . . There are probably some there, your RAS has filtered them out as you choose to concentrate on this book. Until I mention it, you are probably not conscious of the big toe on your right foot. It's there, it's always been there. Once again, the RAS has filtered information coming to your brain from the foot as unnecessary, unimportant, whatever.

This is of great service to us on a number of levels. Imagine how much of a sensory overload the world would be if we did not have the ability to select what information we are consciously aware of.

I have spent the odd hour in a sensory deprivation tank, a float tank. They are sometimes located at beauty/massage places. You go into a small room with your swimmers on, have a shower, and then lie down in a tank that is partially filled with salt water so high in salt content that you float. You put earplugs in and close the lid. No light, no sound, no sense of gravity. Wow. To some people I'm sure it sounds like a form of torture and yet it can be very relaxing, very refreshing, and very rejuvenating.

While you are there, your senses get a rest. The first time I gave one of these a go, the person who worked at the place recommended that, after I had come out of the tank, had a shower and got dressed, I should sit in a room they had set up with a couch, low lights, tea and coffee, and a fish tank. I initially thought to myself, What on earth would I want to do that for? After I've finished my float I have things to do, places to go.

After I came out of the shower and got dressed, the thought of sitting quietly in front of a fish tank having a cup of tea was most attractive. My senses needed to be gently awoken. Even after sitting in front of the fish tank for about 20 minutes, I exited the place onto a busy street and immediately noticed the intensity of light, color, sound that is our everyday experience.

It took a while for the RAS to completely kick in.

RAS Your Résumés

The RAS can also be of great service to us at work. Imagine how much more you would get done in a day if you could manage your RAS to filter out unnecessary information.

Imagine how quickly you will be able to sort through résumés with an RAS that is focused on seeing certain words.

Try this.

I want you to think of the word "you." Hear it sound in your head, hear someone else say it, hear yourself say it. Think of the word "you" in terms of how it looks, the shape of the letters in various fonts, how the word looks when surrounded by other words, when it is a part of larger words like "your" and "you're," how it looks when it is very small and how it looks when it is large and can take up the whole page. Think about the word "you."

Now with the word "you" clearly in your RAS, clearly in your mind, pick a page in this book at random and quickly pass your eyes over the page and watch the word "you" jump out at you.

Before tackling all the résumés that you have sourced through your various means, you can "plug in" your Key Selection Criteria into your RAS in a similar way.

CHAPTER 4

Interview Preparation

Key Selection Criteria and Question Choice

This is where the average manager/recruiter will spend most of their preparation time—question selection. They will have a list of dozens and dozens of questions to ask the candidate. This is fine if average is good enough for you.

The precision recruiter knows that the skill of determining the suitability of the candidate is more in the listening and the follow-up questions than it is in the volume of prepared questions. In fact, having more than 20 prepared questions can result in shifting the focus in the interview from listening to the response to asking the questions.

I have seen some recruiters, supposedly professional ones at that, work their way through a list of 50 questions ticking off each question as they ask it rather than noting down the response from the candidate. Ouch! And organizations pay how much for recruitment consultants?

By the same token, I know some professional recruiters are well aware of the importance of focusing on the listening in an interview. Some of the better consultants will, when appropriate, ask candidates to prepare a written assignment addressing up to three of the Key Selection Criteria. This allows the interview to get to a deeper level quicker and also tests some of the candidate's ability to communicate ideas in a written format.

A good rule of thumb is to have up to three questions per Key Selection Criteria. You may not need to ask all of them for a single Key Selection Criteria.

We will spend a good deal of time later in the book looking at follow-up questions and listening. Take a moment now to turn to Chapter 9: Job aids, reference documents, and freebies. In the Appendices at the end of the book you will find a document entitled, "A Library of

Interview Questions," which provides suggested questions that will help you identify a candidate's preference when it comes to some of the softer skills you might be looking for.

You will also notice that many of them are structured in such a way as to not give away what the question is trying to uncover. Notice the difference between:

Dead giveaway question	Skillfully crafted question
We are looking for a team player. Are you a team player?	Describe to me what the ideal working environment for you would include and exclude?
Have you had any experience with marketing?	Let's say that you have a well-developed brand that has a new product. How would you take the new product to the market place?
What is your work ethic like?	What was one of your major achievements?

Using this list of interview questions, use the space provided here to start to practice linking questions to the Key Selection Criteria for your own example position:

Key Selection Criteria	Questions that could be asked
Key Selection Criteria 1:	
Key Selection Criteria 2:	
Key Selection Criteria 3:	
Key Selection Criteria 4:	
Key Selection Criteria 5:	

Remember that the aim is not to ensure that you ask everyone all of your questions. Rather, the aim is to be able to identify what the candidate will be like to work with in the Key Selection Criteria areas.

Are You Sending the Best Message?

Imagine that you have applied for a job with an organization and you have been selected to attend an interview. Assume that you arrived on time and notice what you are thinking or feeling about working for this organization, as you read through the following scenario.

The receptionist looks at you blankly when you tell her that you are here for an interview for a job and lifts the phone, calls Human Resources and says, "I have someone in reception that says they are here for an interview. Do you know anything about that?"

After Human Resources confirm that there are interviews being held today, the receptionist says, "Take a seat and they'll be down in a minute."

Thirty minutes later, a person comes down and apologizes for the delay and says, "You caught us all a bit by surprise today. The manager that was meant to interview you had double booked and is trying to get out of a meeting as we speak."

They escort you to the manager's office and ask you to wait there. You look around the office and notice that the desk is difficult to see due to all the files, folders, and paper on the desk. The office is very small and seems even more cramped due to a large bookshelf with dozens of folders and books. The computer screen has a rolling marque screen saver saying, "Same s**t, different day."

You can see and hear into the office area outside and the person who showed you in to the office is involved in a lengthy discussion with a team member about a run in they had had yesterday with one of the general managers. The team member who is listening seems all too eager to agree and add their two cents' worth about how just last week that very same general manager said something to them that was so rude. The phone rings in the background and is not answered by either person until they have finished what they were saying . . . well into the eighth ring.

After another 20 minutes a flustered interviewer enters the office and says, "Oh! They didn't put you in the meeting room? You are meant to be in the meeting room."

In the space below write down what you are thinking or feeling about what it would be like to work for this organization.

Now contrast that response with what you would be thinking or feeling about working for this organization if you arrived on time and the following took place.

The receptionist greets you warmly and professionally and asks you to take a seat while they contact Mrs. Saunders who is the person you will be meeting with today.

As soon as the receptionist hangs up the phone they tell you that Penny, Mrs. Saunders' assistant will be down in a moment to introduce herself and take you to the meeting room on Level 2.

No sooner has the receptionist finished explaining that, than Penny arrives, introduces herself, asks if you found a parking spot OK. She then escorts you to Level 2. As you pass reception, the receptionist wishes you good luck.

In the lift Penny makes light conversation about going for interviews, finding the right job and how great it is when you find somewhere you are happy to work.

As she ushers you into the meeting room she tells you that Mrs. Saunders is on her way and offers you tea, coffee or a cool drink. Mrs. Saunders arrives and she shares a smile and a laugh with Penny and then greets you with a firm shake of the hand, a warm smile and says, "Hello you must be (insert your name here). I've been looking forward to meeting you particularly after reading that you have an interest in (insert your favorite hobby here) on your résumé. When did you develop an interest in that?"

In the space below write down what you would be thinking or feeling about what it would be like to work for this organization.

If you want to attract the right person to your organization you will need to consider the quality of every point of contact with the candidate.

CHAPTER 5

Interviews

Creating the Right Environment

Testing or Building Rapport?

In some organizations, there is a trend in interviewing techniques. This is to run the interview like a test. Often there are three or four interviewers in a panel setup. Questions are fired off randomly at the candidate. The direction of the questions chops and changes in order to test the candidate. The person who gets selected for the job is the one who performs best in this environment. The person with the best interview style got the job, not necessarily the best person for the job.

I'll never forget running an interview with a national sales manager. We were looking for a state sales manager and had narrowed the field down to two final candidates. The national sales manager was very skilled at building rapport with a wide range of people. He had built rapport very well with both candidates.

We were in the final interviews and finding it tough to choose when the national sales manager asked one of the candidates, "What's your management style like?"

The candidate replied, "Oh well, you know. It changes dependent on who you're managing."

"What do you mean?" probed the national sales manager.

"Well you know. You have to manage the girls differently to the blokes."

Of course, in an equal employment opportunity company, this response was unacceptable.

The national sales manager had managed to create an environment where the candidate felt so relaxed that they let their "practiced interview technique" guard down. It was more like having a beer at the pub than an interview and as a result we started to see who they really were and what they would be like to work with.

Imagine how useful it would be to see through the "practiced interview technique." Imagine how much time, effort, and money you would save if you could get beyond the "I know what you are going to ask me and I have the perfect answer ready to go." Imagine how precise your recruitment decisions would be if you could know what a person would be like to work with before you had offered them the job.

In order to do this, we need to take a step away from the "test/panel" approach to interviewing and learn how to build unconscious rapport with conscious intent.

How to Build Rapport

We build rapport with someone when we like each other. Have you noticed how people in deep rapport seem to have the same posture, to stand and/or sit in a similar fashion? Sometimes they even dress the same, speak similarly—or have the same type of laugh. This is not an accident! People achieve rapport when the differences between them are minimized and the similarities between them have been maximized. Anyone who has seen the film *Single White Female* will remember a version of this that goes scarily too far.

You are at a party. You have just been introduced to someone and then the person who introduced you has left you to talk. The conversation might go something like.

> *You:* "Where do you live?"
> *Them:* "Up north. A little place called Macaulay. No one's ever heard of it. It's near Sheppard's Mountain. Why? Where do you live?"
> *You:* "Down south. A long way from Sheppard's Mountain."

Nothing in common there. The conversation teeters on the edge of extinction. You try again.

> *You:* "So. Do you play a sport?"
> *Them:* "No. I've never been very sporty."
> *You:* "Oh! I quite like sport."

Now we are really struggling. Unless we find something in common soon, we will both be searching for a reason to leave each other's riveting company and never run into them again. You give it one last shot.

> *You:* "So where do you work?"
> *Them:* "At a software company called Envirotec Solutions."
> *You:* "I know Envirotec Solutions. I did some work for them last year."
> *Them:* "Oh. Really. Who was your contact there?"
> *You:* "Gerry Freeman. He was the . . ."
> *Them:* " . . . General Manager of Service. Everyone knows Gerry. He's great to work with."

Now that you have found something in common, the conversation changes dramatically. The words come more easily, the conversation lightens, the tone changes, the body language improves . . . you start to build rapport.

Not only does this happen on a verbal level, it also happens on many other levels as well.

Why Build Rapport?

From studies in the area of modeling human behavior, it is suggested that when strong influence and liking patterns are at work, rapport is being built at a deep unconscious level. Therefore, to access states of *being liked*, or to effect useful outcomes in business, we can employ the skills of building unconscious rapport, with conscious intent.

The other person or persons will not notice. They will simply feel more at ease with you more quickly, especially if you are very *unlike* them in the first place. It is important to note that the person does not have to like you or be a friend of yours to have rapport—particularly in a professional context.

How Building Rapport Works

The basic principle of rapport is to pace the other person by meeting them where they are. This means understanding each other's values and matching physiology/posture/voice tone and even language style

At an unconscious level, when there is deep rapport, there is a minimization of differences and a move toward sameness.

To turn rapport building into a skill, you can learn to create as much sameness as possible and minimize differences by using a technique known as matching and mirroring.

Matching and Mirroring

This technique involves noticing some part of another person's ongoing experience and doing something the same (mirroring) or something similar (matching).

For example, if the person was sitting swinging a leg, you could sit the same way and swing a leg at the same rate to build sameness, and therefore create rapport (mirroring). Or you could move your hand or finger at the same pace to build tempo and movement sameness and therefore create rapport (matching).

I have not just made this up. This comes from research done by behavioral scientists,* which showed that some people are able to build rapport quicker and better than others. I'm sure we all know some socially challenged people. If you think about it, you will probably notice that they are people who are quite unlike you in many ways. They may be physically very different, they may think differently on issues that are important to you or they may mismatch, rather than match, what you say. You say it's black, they say it's white. You say it's great, they say it's dreadful. You say it's on, they say it's off.

Behavioral scientists observed people who built rapport well and people who did not build rapport well and noticed their different behaviors. The people who built rapport well would naturally match and mirror unconsciously. Next time you are at a social function, dinner party, or BBQ, look around you and notice the people who are getting on really well. I bet there are more similarities than differences.

---

*See: D.S. Sandhu, T.P. Reeves, and R. Pedro. April 1933. "Cross Cultural Counselling and Neurolinguistic Mirroring." *Journal of Multicultural Counselling and Development* 21, no. 2, pp. 106–108; Forster Jansen Margenrot Unterberger (1993).

Some people get a little nervy at this stage. They are probably thinking things like, "Rod. Come on. I liked your other stuff about tips for handling responses and thinking about the big picture and all that. But really! This sounds just a little manipulative."

In response I will use the same argument as the gun lobbyists use. It is not the gun that kills. It is the intention of the user that kills. It is the same here. It is not the skill that is manipulative.

If your intention when using this skill is to manipulate—then it is you who are being manipulative and not the skill. If, however, your intention is to build rapport with the person so that:

- You get beyond the polished interview technique and find out as much as possible about who they really are.
- They feel comfortable, relaxed, and can perform at their best in the interview.
- You increase the likelihood that you are able to put the right person in the right job first time . . .

. . . then I would say that your intention is a good one and the skill, if used well, will support you.

Some Areas to Match and Mirror

- Physiology
  - posture
  - breathing
  - gestures
  - pulse rate
  - overall muscle tension
  - rhythmic movements of limbs, head
  - "energy"
- Voice
  - tone
  - tempo
  - rhythms
  - pitch

- Language
  - visual, auditory, kinesthetic and unspecified predicates
  - jargon
  - repetitive phrases or patterns

Now, I can understand that you might be looking at that list and thinking, "Are you saying that in an interview I should match and mirror their breathing and pulse rate?"

Yes, it will be a little difficult to explain it to the sexual harassment court and I will not accept any responsibility for your misusing this tool. Consider this story, however.

I was running a training course for an organization where we were looking at the issue of how to build rapport. We had completed a couple of activities that basically allowed people to experience the difference between someone mismatching them and then matching them. While debriefing the activity, we were talking about all of the areas where it is possible to match and mirror including pulse rate and breathing.

It was a two-day course and so on the second day, one of the participants came up to me and said,

Rod. That rapport stuff is amazing. I thought I would test it last night. So I hopped into bed next to my wife and began to pace her breathing. I did this for at least two minutes which seemed like a really long time when you are just concentrating on breathing. Then after I was pretty sure that we were in sync, I started to speed it up a little and then start to breath deeper and deeper and faster and faster and next thing you know . . . we were having a bit of a snog.

So please do not just believe me. I strongly recommend that you conduct your own highly scientific experiments in strictly controlled conditions as that highly devoted participant did.

Remember, building rapport is not about copying the other person. It involves the subtle use of these influence patterns. Mimicry or copying can break rapport, so practice carefully and notice others around you. When there is natural rapport, you will find matching and mirroring occurring naturally, completely out of their awareness.

So in an interview you can build rapport with someone by:

- Asking them about a common sport, hobby, or interest listed on their résumé
- Asking them about an organization that you both may have worked for
- Asking them about a person in the industry that you both may know
- Asking them about a similar position that both of you have held
- Talking about a common area where you both live or have lived
- Talking about a name you have in common
- Just talking about anything you have or even have had in common
- Sitting in a similar fashion
- Talking at a similar pace and volume
- Matching their energy levels—are they reserved or are they energetic?
- Using the same jargon
- Nodding in agreement and showing understanding
- Reflecting the same emotion on your face.

Your Opening Comments

After you have built a degree of rapport with the ideas mentioned, you will need to start the formal part of the interview in an informal manner. Once again there is a skill here that distinguishes the average from the precision recruiter.

Imagine what the game of tennis would be like if there were no court markings and no net. What would the game of Aussie Rules be like if there were no goal posts? Or what about soccer if there were no rules?

You wouldn't know if the ball was in or out. Or whether you should play the ball or not. Or even which direction to move in and what to do and not do. Without certain boundaries and rules these, and all other sports, become pointless.

Have you ever been to a meeting that was pointless? Have you ever been to a meeting that lasted far longer than it was initially advertised to last and at the end of it you left even more dazed and confused than when you arrived? Have you ever been to a meeting that had no direction and you did not know whether the discussion was on target or not?

Why does that happen? Often it is because people fail to establish the ground rules at the beginning of the meeting. The chairperson or facilitator or meeting convener often assumes that people have played the game before and know the direction and the point of the meeting. Consequently, they say nothing to set the scene and then no one is quite sure of how to play.

This is also what happens at interviews sometimes. People conducting an interview sometimes walk out of it without all the information they need and wondering why it seems to be so difficult to compare candidates. To avoid this, make sure that your interviews have a clearly stated point and direction. You are in charge of the interview and you are responsible for obtaining a certain amount, and a certain type, of information necessary to make a precision decision.

To do this you can use a skill called framing . . .

Framing Skills

The skill of framing is primarily a verbal skill that, when used well, has the following benefits. Framing:

- Increases the likelihood that you will achieve what you set out to achieve
- Reduces the amount of wastage
- Increases your level of professionalism
- Increases the likelihood that other people in the interview will follow your lead
- Earns permission from others in the interview for you to do what you need to do
- Prepares other people in the interview for what you will be asking of them
- Increases the likelihood that the other people in the interview will comply with requests.

Here are some sample frames. As you read through them, imagine you were on the receiving end of the frames. Contrast your response if you were in the same situation and received no frame from the other person before they launched in.

Presentation Frame

*allows you to present something without being
interrupted*

*'I'd like to take a couple of minutes
to explain the organisation and the position.'*

Time Frame

*establishes expectations
around when to stop the
interview*

*'I expect we will finish up
before 11am.'*

Backtrack Frame

*use this to regain
rapport or to
confirm understanding*

*'Can I just go
over that again
to confirm what
was said?'*

Questioning Frame

*helps when you
need to uncover information*

*'Is it OK if I ask you a few questions
to get a clear understanding
of how you see
the situation?'*

Process Frame

helps set the agenda for the interview

*'The way I'd like to run this
interview is…'*

Closing Frame

*Good for bringing the
interview to an end
- especially useful
for those who tend to go on
and on and on …*

'So, in closing …'
or
*'Perhaps I can finish up by
outlining the next
steps for us…'*

Framing an Interview

When opening an interview there are several frames in a certain order that will dramatically improve your interviews:

Interview Process Frame

> Chris, the way we'd like to run the interview is this.
>
> Firstly for me to give you a brief overview of the organization, the division in which the vacancy exists and a little about the position that we are looking to fill.
>
> After that we will be asking you a few questions to find out as much as we can about you, your experience and expertise and suitability for the position.
>
> Thirdly, as we go through the interview there may be some questions that you have come to mind. If so, please ask them as they occur to you and we will also have some time later in the interview to answer any final or prepared questions you might have. The aim is to do our best to ensure you leave here with a crystal clear understanding of what it is like to work here and how suited you would be.
>
> And then finally we will summarize what we have covered and discuss what the next steps are.
>
> All of this should take about an hour. How does that sound?

Overview Frame

So let me start by providing you with an overview of the organization, the division in which the vacancy exists and a little about the position that we are looking to fill.

Questioning Frame

I'd like to ask you a number of different types of questions today. Some will be about your experience and expertise and others will be about what sort of work and environment you need to perform at your best.

So here is the first question . . .

Your Questions Frame

Well that's all the questions I have at this stage. Perhaps as we were going through there were questions you thought of or perhaps you have some prepared questions that you would like to ask now.

Feedback Frame

Rather than you leave here without any indication as to how you went, what I'd like to do is quickly identify some areas I noticed that will help you if you are successful and some areas that would be a challenge to you if you were successful. The first thing I noticed was . . .

Next Steps Frame

The process for us from here on in is . . .

Outlining the Job without Giving Away the Answers

When a candidate starts asking questions about the organization, the division, the work, and your job, an average interviewer will talk too long and give too much away. Enjoying the sound of their own voice and the feeling of talking about something that the other person does not know and is interested in is an easy trap.

All the candidate needs to do is listen closely and then throw your words back at you, surrounded by slightly different ones and somehow they seem like the perfect person for the job. All they have really done is shown good comprehension and reflection skills.

A precision recruiter will avoid the seductive feeling of being the expert and give the interviewee enough to keep them happy but not enough to give away the answers to their questions.

The following three things will help you here.

Rehearsal

Prepare what you will say before you say it. Otherwise the last candidate that you interview will get the best version and the first candidate that you interview will get a very inarticulate, confused version.

Maximum Time

Set yourself a maximum time for the overview. Try to stick to a maximum of 5 minutes. This is usually enough to satisfy initial questions from the candidate and yet not enough to give them the answers to your questions.

Three Levels

A useful template to use for your overview is to talk about things on three levels:

A) The organization
B) The department/division
C) The position

Here's an Example . . .

"Impact" is a boutique training organization that provides high-quality learning and development solutions to client organizations. We work closely with the client to truly understand their business from market forces, strategic, and internal issues perspectives. Then we use this understanding to design and deliver targeted learning and development solutions.

The marketing and sales division is responsible for profile building, through lead generation and to lead conversion. We are proud of our record in maintaining and developing current clients as well as finding new clients.

The position of business development manager is a central and exciting role reporting straight to the national sales and marketing manager. It involves market analysis, design of marketing initiatives, and lead generation. The successful applicant will assist the facilitators with lead conversion. The salary package is designed to both guarantee a degree of security while also providing attractive incentives for solid performance.

That's all I'll say at the moment. If you have any other questions regarding the details of the position, we can discuss them later in the interview.

CHAPTER 6

Advanced Questioning Skills

Legal and Illegal Questions

Have you ever asked any of the following questions in an interview:

- How old are you?
- Are you married?
- How many children do you have?
- Where were you born?
- Do you have a partner?

Many of these questions are asked by interviewers trying to build some degree of rapport or trying to make the candidate, and themselves, more comfortable. They are illegal. Why? Because they have no bearing on the person's ability to do the job you are asking them to do.

There are some key principles that will help determine whether your questions are legal or illegal. Would you ask the same question if you were interviewing:

- a woman?
- a man?
- an older person?
- a younger person?
- a Caucasian?
- a non-Australian-born citizen
- an Australian-born citizen?
- a physically able person?
- someone dressed in a suit?

If worst comes to worst and a rejected candidate takes you to court for discrimination, you will be required to prove that:

- the question directly related to the ability of the person to carry out the duties of the position
- you did ask every candidate the same question.

Hard as it is to believe, I still meet people who believe that whether a woman has had children yet or not is directly related to their ability to do the job or not. It must be so hard living in a world where the values are years ahead of your beliefs and behaviors!!!

Oh well, enough judgment. Here is a sample list of illegal questions.

How Old Are You?

This question is not legal. Federal and State laws prohibit age discrimination. It is a good idea to avoid focusing on age, except in those cases where an occupation requires extraordinary physical ability or training and a valid age-related rule is in effect. This information can also usually be obtained from a resume.

This Is a Hectic Office. Can You Keep Up With the Younger People Here?

This question is illegal as stated; it indicates a possible age bias. However, it could be reworded as "How would you describe the way you manage stress/deal with a rapid pace in an organizational setting?"

Have You Ever Been Arrested?

This question is illegal unless an inquiry about arrests is justified by the specific nature of the business. Questions about arrests are generally considered suspect since they may tend to disqualify minority groups. Convictions should be the basis for rejection of an applicant only if their number, their nature, or how recent they are render the applicant unsuitable. The interviewer should tell the applicant that a conviction record should not necessarily preclude employment.

Have You Ever Been Convicted of a Crime?

This question is legal but might be inadvisable. (In most cases, convictions are a matter of public record.) The question is advisable if conviction of a crime in and of itself is relevant to employment but the interviewer should be aware that on a number of occasions it has been perceived as conveying a prejudice against minorities. An important point, too, is that being arrested (held in custody) is not the same as being convicted (proven guilty after a legal trial).

Do You Have Any Disabilities?

This question is illegal as phrased here. An applicant does not have to divulge handicaps or health conditions that do not relate reasonably to his or her fitness to perform the job.

Are You Married?

This question is illegal and should not be reworded. Marriage has nothing directly to do with job performance. In addition, the question might have sexual overtones or might imply a prejudice for or against a particular marital status or sexuality.

Do You Have Children, and If You Do, What Kind of Child Care Arrangements Do You Have?

Both parts of this question are inappropriate; they should not be asked in any form because the answers are not job-related.

Instead you could ask the question, "We often have to work Saturdays, at least once a month, and sometimes late nights. Would that present any problems for you?"

Please note: This question, if asked, needs to be directed to both males and females.

Where Were You Born?

This question is illegal and should not be reworded. There is no legal reason for asking it, and it might indicate discrimination on the basis of national origin.

Do You Get along Well With Other Men/Women?

This question is illegal; it seems to perpetuate sexism. However, if the objective in asking it is to determine whether the applicant gets along well with people in general, the question might be reworded as "How would you describe your style of communication with others?" or "How would you describe your leadership style?"

What Languages Can You Speak and/or Write Fluently?

Although this question is legal, it might be perceived as a sly way of determining an individual's national origin. However, it is permissible to ask the question if the job involves language ability (for example, when the job of a salesperson requires dealing primarily with customers who seek a particular language). It is not permissible to ask how any given language was learned.

What Experience, If Any, Have You Had in the Armed Forces?

This question is legal if the purpose is to discover job-related skills or knowledge that may have been learned in the armed forces but questions about the specific skills or knowledge would be preferable.

Do You Have Any Medical Problems That Would Prevent You from Performing Your Job Duties?

This question is legal. It is permissible to ask about general or specific conditions of a physical, mental, or medical nature if those conditions would interfere with the applicant's ability to perform the job.

What Experience Have You Had in . . .?

This question is legal as long as it is job-related.

More Than Just Open and Closed Questions

Have you ever noticed how just about every TAFE course and many business-related university courses seem to have a Business

Communication module? I reckon that you could be doing a "Bonsai Your Pet" course, a "Self-actualization through Macramé" course, or a "Creative Tooth Decay" course at your local community college and each one will include a Business Communication component.

OK, I agree there is obviously a high degree of importance around being able to communicate effectively in the workplace. If you have ever done one of these courses, you probably would have covered the topic of questions. And you would more than likely be aware that there are two types of questions very commonly referred to: open and closed questions.

What Are Open and Closed Questions?

Closed questions are questions that require a "yes" or "no" response. Open questions are questions that require a more detailed response than yes or no.

How to Start the Question

The words that we use at the beginning of a question will determine whether the question is an open question or a closed question:

Closed	Open
Do/Don't	Why
Did/Didn't	What
Will/ Won't	How
Was/Wasn't	
Would/Wouldn't	
Could/Couldn't	
Should/Shouldn't	
Is/Isn't	
Are/Aren't	

Questions that start with When, Where, and Who are strictly speaking open questions. Yet, for all intents and purposes they tend to elicit more of a closed-type response.

When? The late 1990s.
Where? The Oval Office.
Who? Monica Lewinsky.

So from a practical perspective these words are also considered to be starting a closed question.

Even if we use words like "tell me" or "describe" there will be an implied or overt "why," "what" or "how" after it. Tell me why . . . , describe how . . .

Celebrity Head

If you have ever played the game celebrity head, you will have experienced the difference between open and closed questions. One person has the name of a famous person stuck to their forehead or stuck to their back and they need to determine who they are. They can only ask closed questions to do this.

"Am I still alive?" "Was I a good person?" "Did I act in movies?"

Closed questions are low on information. It takes a long time to determine the answer to something using only closed questions.

Open questions are high on information. If you ask an open question, the person who is answering the question gets to take the answer wherever they want to go. And this can be a limitation of open questions. You sacrifice control of the response for increased information. With closed questions you sacrifice information and yet you have complete control over the direction of the questioning process.

Content or Context?

Now, of course, we cannot guarantee that just because we ask a question using a certain word at the beginning that people will answer it a certain way. A person's response has a lot to do with their preference for content or context.

For example, you might ask a friend who had just seen a movie, "How was the movie?"

Someone who has a preference for content responses might answer by saying, "Yeah good." Anyone with teenagers will know what this is like.

"How was your day at school son?"
"OK."
"What did you do?"
"Nothing."
"Are you seeing Holly this weekend?"
"Maybe."

Someone who has a preference for context responses might answer by saying,

> Well, I haven't seen a movie with Bruce Willis in it for some time, so I was quite surprised by his performance in comparison to the Die Hard film. I though in the Die Hard films he was a bit type cast. I must admit because of that I was a bit reluctant to see this one. But when Evan and his wife said they were going, I thought that it would be nice to meet Evan's wife and have a bit of dinner . . .

A smart interviewer will recognize the preferred response type that the candidate has, content or context, and will adjust the amount of open or closed questions accordingly.

So in Summary

Closed	Open
A definition: *Questions that require a 'yes' or 'no' response.*	A definition: *Questions that require a more detailed response than yes or no.*
Words to start a closed question include: Do/Don't Did/Didn't Will/Won't Was/Wasn't Would/Wouldn't Could/Couldn't Should/Shouldn't Is/Isn't Are/Aren't When/Where/Who	**Words to start an open question:** Why What How Tell me Describe
Benefits/drawbacks: Low on information High on control	**Benefits/drawbacks:** High on information Low on control
Content or context tactic: If you are getting content responses reduce the number of closed questions. If you are getting context responses increase the number of closed questions.	**Content or context tactic:** If you are getting content responses increase the number of open questions. If you are getting context responses reduce the number of open questions.

Fluff Busting

Open and closed questions are not enough. By themselves there is still too much room for miscommunication. Try this activity:

In the following space write down the first five words that you associate with the word "learning:"

Now in the following space write down the first five words you associate with the word "sex:"

Compare the words you wrote to the words that I wrote and let's see how many words we had exactly the same.

Learning: Career, School, Activity, Test, Play

Sex: Margaret, Fun, happy, Birth, Batman suit.

How many did we have the same?

Not many, I'll bet. In fact I'd take out a mortgage size loan to bet money on the fact if you did this activity as instructed and without looking at my responses then we would not even have three words exactly the same.

Why is this? We both use the same language and yet the words within that language all exist within our own perception. We use the same words and yet the images that come to mind, the other words that we associate with and the feelings we get, are all individual images, associations, and feelings.

Problems can arise in an interview if you only ask open and closed questions. There is still too much room for a difference in interpretation. And this difference can result in your having to manage poor performance from the candidate you selected or, worse still, that you have to manage them out of the organization within a year of them being recruited.

Fortunately there is a further questioning skill that will help here. It is called fluff busting.

If you want to find out what another human being really means by their communication and how their thought processes are affecting their behavior, the following five questions can "point" you in the right direction. These "Pointers"* are very powerful tools, and need to be used sensitively and respectfully.

Pointer 1: Nouns

Dictionaries do not define words absolutely. The meanings of words are modified by our past experiences and our future expectations. Any particular noun has as many definitions as there are people using the noun.

The Pointer to use when you are confronted with fluffy nouns is, "What specifically?"

For example, your candidate says, "I want a new job."

. . . you can bust the fluff with, "What job, specifically?"

Even if you can make a good guess, do not count on this guess.

Pointer 2: Verbs

When confronted with a "fluffy" verb, use the second Pointer, "How specifically?"

For example, your candidate says, "I implemented the project."

. . . you can bust the fluff with, "How exactly did you go about the implementation?"

Pointer 3: Rules

People have rules for themselves. Words that indicate that someone is referring to a rule are "should," "shouldn't," "must," "mustn't," "have to," "can't," "ought" and so on. These words indicate rules that may or may not be legitimate. Rules are useful in some situations. They stop us from hurting each other and ourselves. Sometimes rules are fences that limit

---

*The name 'Pointer' comes from Genie Laborde's book, Influencing with Integrity, Management Skills for Communication & Negotiation, Genie z. Laborde, 1987 Syntony Publishing. ISBN 0 933347 10 3.

our possibilities. When confronted by a rule it is often useful to test the rule to find out why it exists, how this person builds rules for themselves, and to expand the limit of their thinking.

There was an excellent example of this on television a number of years ago. In North Sydney you would occasionally find police booking people for jaywalking at lunchtime, crossing before the pedestrian lights had turned green. The police would call the pedestrian to one side, inform them they had just jaywalked. The police would say they needed to write a ticket and ask the pedestrian for their personal details.

The incident got coverage on the news one night, showing a woman who tested the rules perfectly. She had crossed the road against the pedestrian lights and a policeman informed her of her indiscretion and said, "I'm going to have to book you for jaywalking. Can I have your name and address please?"

The woman replied, "What would happen if I didn't give you my name and address and I just walked off?"

The policeman said, "Nothing, madam. I can't arrest you for jaywalking."

So she said, "Fine. See you later." And walked off.

The statement that challenges "should," "must," and "have to" statements is: "What would happen if you didn't?" Conversely, the way to challenge the "shouldn't," "mustn't," and "can't" statements is with "What would happen if you did?"

So in an interview, your candidate says: "You should manage the process in that order."

. . . you can bust the fluff with, "What would happen if you didn't manage it that way?"

The Rules Pointer must be used sensitively! People do not take kindly to having the limitations in their thinking exposed.

Pointer 4: Generalizations

To expose the fallacy of generalizations such as "never," "always," "everyone," "all," "they" and so on, use the Generalization Pointer.

Few generalizations are true *all* the time. When we generalize, we ignore the "exceptions to the rule." Generalizations can be limiting, blocking off unexamined or unnoticed solutions to problems.

An example is if someone says, "They say his assistants never last long." By finding out who "they" are to check out the generalization, you may discover that the "reliable source" is in fact the coffee vendor who only started the job last week.

Similarly, your candidate may say something like, "All managers have an autocratic streak."

There are actually two ways to bust the fluff here.

The first requires a good deal of rapport as it can come across as a little harsh. You can repeat the generalization back to them with a big question mark at the end. "All?" "Every?" "Never?"

The softer way is to ask the candidate if they can think of an example or a context where the generalization is not true. "Can you think of a manager you have met or worked with that did not have an autocratic streak?"

Pointer 5: Comparisons

This Pointer is used when what is being compared is not immediately obvious. For example, if people use the words "better," "worse," "easier," "nice," "enough" and so on, they are making a comparison of some sort. They themselves may not be aware of the comparison.

If your candidate says, "It's better to do it the way we did it."

You can bust the fluff by asking, "Better than what way?"

An Excellent Role Model for Questioning

You might remember the TV series Detective Colombo that started in the 1970s and was still being played in the early 1990s. You could probably still see reruns on pay TV.

With Detective Colombo you were pretty certain who committed the murder from before the first add break. It wasn't so much whodunnit, the thrust of the show was more how he worked it out.

You would see a dead body on the floor, in a partially lit, well-appointed house. The camera would then pan across the scene to reveal signs of a struggle and then you would focus on a figure. You could not make out the details, but you could see a cufflink, a cigarette, something that would lead you in a certain direction just before the ad break.

When you came back from the break, it would be the same well-appointed house, but in the day time and the police are all around the room searching for evidence, photographing the body. And then the camera pans across again, and there is a man, smoking a cigarette and wearing the same cufflinks!

In comes Detective Colombo with his glass eye, his Bronx accent, his cigar, and the trench coat that seems too heavy for him. After some initial enquiries he starts to interview the man smoking the cigarette. And he uses the above model to perfection.

Colombo:	"So what were you doing last night?" (Open question)
Cigarette-smoking suspect:	"I'm afraid I'm not going to be of much use to you Detective, you see I was having dinner with friends."
Colombo:	"Where exactly were you having dinner?" "Who specifically was there with you?" "What time did you leave?" "When did you arrive here and find the body?" "How did you travel here?" "What route did you take?" (Fluff busting)
Colombo:	"So let me get this straight. Am I correct in thinking that you left dinner with the senator at 10.30 and came straight here? Is that correct?" (Closed question)
Colombo:	"What did you find when you arrived?" (Back to the open questions)
Cigarette-smoking suspect:	"I found it exactly as you see it now."

Colombo:	"Exactly?"
	"Can you think of anything in the room that is different to when you first entered?"
	"How many cigarettes specifically?"
	"What brand do you smoke?"
	(Fluff Busting)
Colombo:	"So let me get this straight. Am I correct in thinking that the police have moved the lamp and you have smoked two cigarettes since you first arrived?" (Closed question)

The Fluff-busting Monster

And so it would continue until the cigarette-smoking suspect would start to get very uncomfortable and usher Detective Colombo to the door with the excuse of a very important meeting that they needed to attend and prepare for.

Colombo would shuffle toward the door, hesitate on the doorstep and turn round, saying,

"One more thing . . ."
"I was just wondering . . ."
"I found myself asking . . ."
"Something I'm not sure of . . ." "I'm curious to know . . ."
"I'm quite interested in . . ."
"I'd be fascinated to know . . ."
"As you were saying that, I was thinking . . ."
"I would be interested to hear . . ."

These are called softeners as they soften the question-asking process. If you ask fluff-busting questions without them, it can become a harsh process. It's a process that requires a lot of rapport or it will damage the relationship and the goodwill. You become the dreaded fluff-busting monster.

"What do you mean by manage?"

"How exactly did you implement?"

"Better?"

"All?"

"Compared to what?"

Sprinkle a few softeners in there and you create an easier, friendlier, less taxing questioning process.

- "I'm curious to know what you specifically mean when you use the word manage?"
- "That is a real feather in your cap. Well done. I found myself asking how you went about the implementation process?"
- "I was just wondering when you said 'Better,' better than what? Had you done it another way?"
- "Can you think of an example when that was not the case?"
- "Something I'm not sure of is what you are comparing it to when you say difficult?"

Finding a STAR Performer

Behavioral Questioning Skills

Keeping in mind that your job as a recruiter is to find out as much as you can about each candidate, imagine that you are interviewing a candidate and you have asked them the question, "What would you consider to be one of your major achievements?" Notice your thoughts and feelings when they respond with:

Um. Well I got my Graduate Diploma. That was a good achievement.

Now imagine that you are interviewing a candidate and you have asked them the same question: "What would you consider to be one of your major achievements?" Notice your thoughts and feelings when they respond with:

> The situation I found myself in 5 years ago was quite a frustrating one. I had joined the industry with the aim of being able to do the role I'm currently in. I could see a fairly clear path to that role but I had been knocked back for promotion on a couple of occasions.

> So the task, as I saw it, was to identify what was holding me back and then take some action.

> The action I took was to research the position and its requirements. I found that the main requirement I was lacking was postgraduate study in the area. So I enrolled in the course, applied myself to it and the full time job at the same time and finally graduated 3 years later with my Graduate Diploma.

> The result was that, not only had I gained a vast amount of knowledge I did not have before the study but I also was promoted into the position I was looking to get while completing my study.

Obviously, if you accept that your role as a recruiter is to find out as much as you can about this person, the second response is, while probably rehearsed, more useful to us. Many candidates who have been through an outplacement program or attended interview skill training will recognize the behavioral formula to that response.

As recruiters, we need to do two things:
1. Recognize the behavioral, rehearsed response.
2. Evoke it from the candidate if they give us the first response.

The behavioral response is using the STAR formula. There are a number of versions of it but basically STAR stands for:

- Situation
- Task
- Action
- Result

Reread the second response and you will see the different sections and the specific words being used.

"The **situation** I found myself in . . .
"So the **task** as I saw it . . .
"The **action** I took . . .
"The **result** was . . ."

Whether the candidate uses it or not is of little importance. What this tells you about the candidate is that they have prepared, learned, and can implement skills when needed. Although this should not be totally ignored, a precision recruiter would put this into perspective against their Key Selection Criteria.

What is of more use to you as a recruiter is to be able to evoke this response from the candidate if they don't know how to answer interview questions. This is easily done by turning the STAR formula into questions: "I'd be curious to know what the **situation** was before you got your Graduate Diploma that prompted you to think that tertiary study was important enough to devote 3 years to it?"

With that frustration in mind what was the **task** ahead as you saw it then?

So what **action** did you take? As well as enrolling and completing exams what else did you do?

What would you say is the **result** of that? What do you have now that you didn't have before the Graduate Diploma?

You may have noticed that these are all open questions and you could follow up each of these questions with fluff-busting and closed questions. Now you can see, perhaps, why it is unnecessary to prepare more than 10 questions. With all of the follow-up questions you can ask, you will find that there is no shortage of things to talk about.

CHAPTER 7

Advanced Listening Skills

Are You Really Listening or Just Waiting to Talk?

The mind can think hundreds of times faster than anyone can talk. Those of you who know some fast and persistent talkers may doubt this, yet it is true. While many of us are listening to someone talk, our mind is shooting off in a dozen different directions . . . formulating an argument here, drawing conclusions there, and identifying a couple of examples for good measure. And then we are waiting for the other person to draw breath so we can jump in with what our mind has found for us.

This is not listening. It is waiting for your turn to talk. And that is very different. Listening requires a far greater degree of control over your own mind.

Another fantastic thing about the questioning process that we have built using open, fluff-busting, closed, and STAR questions is that in order to use it really well, you have to listen. You have to *really* listen . . . to every word, because you are listening out for pointers to fluff bust or triggers to STAR. You also need to listen really carefully, as you have not prepared the next questions that are dependent on what the candidate says.

A good rule of thumb is that the interview is made up of 80:20. That is, 20 percent of your time in the interview is spent talking and 80 percent is spent listening.

And that is just the basics!

Every Behavior Has an Equal and Opposite

Precision Listening

Have you ever noticed how some salespeople have the knack of making a drawback or limitation of their product sound as though it's a real benefit?

What the salesperson says . . .	What they really mean . . .
"The house is a renovator's dream!"	The house is infested with white ants and should be demolished.
"It's a beautiful car built in the time when cars were what they should be: big, fast, and gutsy."	The car is difficult to park, uneconomical, and you'll have trouble finding replacement parts.
"This comes with our standard three-year warranty."	That's if you can prove conclusively, potentially in a court of law, that the fault was not due to the way you used the product OR the product only lasts about three years, then things start to fall apart!

It is important to remember that the salesperson is not necessarily being deliberately dishonest. They often try to present an aspect of their product in a light that would be attractive to particular people:

- A savvy investor or handy renovator could make a killing on the house.
- The purchaser might be more interested in maintaining and restoring the car as it becomes a vintage car.
- You may only want the product for three years.

In a recruitment interview situation, the same dynamic can happen.

What the candidate says . . .	What could happen when they start work . . .
"I'm a team player! I really enjoy working as part of a team."	The candidate cannot work autonomously. They won't make a move without the team having a meeting and coming to a consensus.
"I take a proactive approach to solving problems."	They are constantly complaining to you and all others in the team about minor issues. They blame others and have no tact. They find things that are not real priorities and waste resources trying to fix them.
"I couldn't get a job for 6 months."	They approach the job with a "whatever it takes" attitude to ensure that they keep the job and become an asset to the organization. They only select a job that they are 100 percent happy with.
"I had to leave because my manager could not see I was right."	They are prepared to stand up for what they believe to be right even if the person they are challenging is their boss.

A precision recruiter knows that there is as much in the listening as there is in the questioning. They are listening to the words chosen and the words avoided. For every behavior there is a context in which that behavior is of less use.

The precision recruiter overlays the words used with the Key Selection Criteria and an understanding of the organization, the division/team, and the role itself. They will also know that if the candidate says they have something as a strength, it means there is a potential weakness as well.

Following are some continuums that suggest what you might be sacrificing when you are looking for something specific.

Able to work as part of a team	Able to work autonomously
Able to think strategically	Able to implement at a practical level
Sensitive to others needs	Able to think logically and clearly
Decisive	Creative
Task focused	People focused
Big picture awareness	Attention to detail
Need to change	Satisfied
Able to plan for all possibilities	Able to deal with the unexpected

Now, I am by no means suggesting that, just because someone says that they are a team player, they have no ability to work autonomously. That, of course, is just not the case. What I *am* saying, however, is that if you listen to the words that a person chooses to describe their experience, you may start to see a pattern. It is the pattern that a precision recruiter would concern themselves with, not a one-off statement. Individually, the words that we use are arbitrary, together there is a pattern.

Imagine that you are interviewing a candidate and you ask them the question, "How would you describe your ideal work environment?"

Now you know about:

- Listening to the words selected to describe their experience
- The continuums given in the previous section
- Behaviors being useful in some contexts

see what you can pick up about potential patterns in this response.

The ideal work environment for me would be one where there are limited interruptions. I really enjoy being able to put my head down and tail up, and produce something of value without interruptions from phones, people walking in for a chat, mobiles going off and so on.

I also tend to perform best when I have clear objectives and know exactly what I need to do to achieve them. I find it most satisfying when there is a well thought out plan that is ticking like clockwork.

Another component of the ideal work environment for me would be challenge. I work best when there is a difficult or complex task that requires some detailed analysis to identify the root cause of the issue rather than dealing with the symptoms. I find that way the solutions implemented are right first time and there is no need to revisit the issue.

You could start to recognize some patterns when we group together the following comments:

". . . limited interruptions . . ."
". . . head down and tail up and produce something . . ."
". . . without interruptions from phones, people walking in for a chat, mobiles going off and so on"
". . . clear objectives and know exactly what I need to do to achieve them."
". . . well thought out plan that is ticking like clockwork."
". . . difficult or complex task . . ."
". . . detailed analysis . . ."
". . . root cause of the issue . . ."
". . . right first time and there is no need to revisit . . ."

Can you recognize some possible preferences for:

- Working autonomously over being part of a team
- Logic and facts over emotion and tact
- Task over people
- Attention to detail over a view of the big picture
- Planning over a preference to deal with the unexpected

Now you are starting to be able to understand what it would be like to work with this person six months down the track. You can start to hear their strengths and potential weaknesses.

You would, of course, being the precision recruiter that you are, follow these patterns up with further questions to help confirm or deny the pattern:

- "Can you think of a time when you were in a job that did have constant interruptions? What did you do? How did you deal with the interruptions?"
- "If I was to ask other people who have worked with you to describe you, what words would they use?"
- "Imagine you have a tight deadline to meet and you are waiting on another person to complete something before you can finalize your component, have everything 100 percent and meet the deadline. How would you convey the sense of urgency to the other person?"
- "Can you think of a time that a plan failed, that the plan did not go according to plan? How did you respond?"

If the patterns still emerge after these questions, chances are you have found a preference . . . and a blind spot.

Overlay these preferences and blind spots with your Key Selection Criteria and you will start to find it very easy to identify whether the candidate is suitable or not.

Closing the Interview—the Next Steps

There are three steps in closing an interview:

1. Providing the candidate with some feedback.
2. Providing the candidate with an overview of the next steps.
3. Leaving the candidate with a positive feeling about the organization.

Providing the Candidate with Some Feedback

Most poor recruiters find this too difficult to do at the end of the interview. They will probably be thinking:

- "But Rod, I don't know if they have got the job or not."
- "But Rod, I will need to check in with the other interviewers."
- "But Rod, What if I have nothing nice to say?"

You do not need to tell them they have the job or not at this stage. You can speak on behalf of yourself and also ensure that other interviewers are able to add their perspectives as well if it is appropriate. And if you have nothing nice to say then you weren't listening well enough!

During the interview look out for two things:

- What you think this candidate has going for them.
- What you think this candidate will find challenging in the role if they are successful.

You can then close the interview this way:

Simone, rather than you leave here without any indication as to how you went, what I'd like to do is to identify some areas I noticed that, if you were successful, will help you some areas that would be a challenge to you.

If you were successful, I think your tenacity and professionalism as outlined in your experience in project managing the customer relationship management initiative would be very valuable. I also think that your experience in the pharmaceutical industry would be very beneficial.

If you were successful, the role may prove very challenging for you with the degree of autonomy required. Another challenge for you in the role could be the level of communication skills that is often expected from our team when making presentations and dealing with difficult clients.

Providing the Candidate with an Overview of the Next Steps

This simple and obvious part of the interview is often left unsaid. You need to ensure that the candidate leaves the interview clearly understanding your decision process. This will reduce the number of unnecessary follow-up calls from candidates and increase the professionalism of your interview.

One way of covering this could be:

Well, I think that is about all for the moment. Our process from here is to continue interviewing a number of other candidates. We will then be meeting to determine who we would like to see at a second interview. You will hear from us toward the end of next week.

Leaving the Candidate with a Positive Feeling about the Organization

There are a number of ways to do this:

- Refer back to the topic you used to build rapport.
- Offer them a freebie or company merchandise.
- Take them on a tour (if appropriate).
- Tell a feel-good story about the company's products or services.
- Refer them to a book, Internet site, or article that is related to what you talked about.

Most industries are incestuous and stories about good and bad experiences spread like stories about good and bad service. This is your opportunity to improve the organization's standing in the industry. A precision recruiter would make the most of it without being too over the top.

CHAPTER 8

After the Interview

Making the Decision as Easy as Possible

When it comes time to making a decision about who would be the best for the job, or even who you would like to see at the next stage of the recruitment process, some of the ideas that we have already covered will make the decision much easier:

At the beginning of the recruitment process:

- Be aware of the clone syndrome.
- Spend time on the recruitment process rather than just putting a bum on a seat.
- Do a gap analysis for the business, your department/division and the position.
- Select Key Selection Criteria for the journey to the desired situation.
- Determine the best recruitment strategy.
- Build an advertisement that attracts the most appropriate candidates.
- Be conscious of sending the best possible message to all candidates at all times.

Around the interview:

- Base the questions you ask in an interview on the Key Selection Criteria.
- Build rapport with the candidates so you are more likely to see what they will be like to work within six months.
- Answer the candidates' questions without giving away the answers to your questions.

- Run a structured yet flexible interview using framing skills.
- Use fluff-busting and behavioral questioning.
- Listen between the lines to the words the candidate uses and avoids.
- Remember that for every behavior there is a context where that behavior will be both a hindrance and a help.

The Decision Analysis Process

Comparing Candidates

If you have done a bit of recruitment in the past, chances are that you will have at some stage found it difficult to make a decision. This candidate is better when it comes to X but the other has it all over them when it comes to Y. A similar form of decision paralysis can happen when there are two or more people involved in the decision process. Whatever the cause, there is a process that will help. I will take you through the process over the following pages.

Step 1: Prioritize and Weight the Key Selection Criteria

List below your Key Selection Criteria in order of importance. Then give each criterion a weighting. The weighting helps differentiate the relative value of each of the Key Selection Criteria. To give a Key Selection Criteria a rating of 3 would be to say that it is of higher value than a Key Selection Criteria of 1 or 2. For example:

Key selection criteria	Weighting
1. Ability to sell and maintain relationships	3
2. Ability to work autonomously	3
3. Product/industry knowledge	2
4. Ability to manage a territory	2
5. Organization and paperwork	1

Step 2: Score and Justify Each Candidate

While you are in the interview, make notes that will help you determine a final score for the candidate for each Key Selection Criteria. As soon as the candidate has left, consolidate your notes and select a final score out of 10 for the candidate in each of the Key Selection Criteria. To continue the example:

Candidate's Name: Leah Hemming

Key selection criteria	Weighting	Score out of 10
1. Ability to sell and maintain relationships Refer sales results from previous role. Response to question on building relationships highlighted natural ability to build rapport.	3	9
2. Ability to work autonomously Three years' experience as representative. In previous role worked in remote territory. Still produced results.	3	8
3. Product/industry knowledge Has not worked in this industry.	2	3
4. Ability to manage a territory Refer to response on taking over a new territory. Resources used in previous role.	2	7
5. Organization and paperwork Dismissive of paperwork.	1	2

Step 3: Do Your Sums

Then do your sums by multiplying the weighting by the score out of 10. This will give you a subtotal for each Key Selection Criteria. Add the total score by adding the subtotals together. You will also need to total the highest possible score as this will not necessarily be 100. To finalize the example:

Candidate's Name: Leah Hemming

Key selection criteria	Weighting	Score out of 10	Subtotal
1. Ability to sell and maintain relationships Refer sales results from previous role. Response to question on building relationships highlighted natural ability to build rapport.	3	9	27/30

(*Continued*)

Key selection criteria	Weighting	Score out of 10	Subtotal
2. Ability to work autonomously Three years' experience as representative. In previous role worked in remote territory. Still produced results.	3	8	24/30
3. Product/industry knowledge Has not worked in this industry.	2	3	6/20
4. Ability to manage a territory Refer to response on taking over a new territory. Resources used in previous role.	2	7	14/20
5. Organization and paperwork Dismissive of paperwork.	1	2	2/10
Totals			73/110

Once you have done this for each candidate, the comparison becomes relatively easy.

Now, I can understand that some of the more scientifically minded people are thinking to themselves that this process is hardly foolproof. Scores are still subjective, comments are still contextual, so this is, at best, pseudo-science.

The thing to remember is that there are no magic-wand approaches when it comes to decision making. There are no 100-percent logical processes to determine who you will hire. We are emotional beings as much as we are logical beings and to think that a totally logical decision is somehow superior is to ignore the idea that many exceptional decisions are made with emotion.

What this process does is keep your Key Selection Criteria in mind, in perspective, and in the right ratio.

Reference Checking

The aim of reference checking is not necessarily to make a final decision about the candidate, it is more to identify:

- *Consistent information:* Information that is consistent between you and several referees obviously bodes well for its validity.
- *Inconsistent information:* Information that is inconsistent does not necessarily mean that someone is wrong. It should, however, highlight the need for some more clarification.
- *New information:* New information should be put into context. Ask yourself how relevant the new information is to your Key Selection Criteria.

As with all other aspects of recruitment, reference checking is one of the steps that a poor recruiter will short cut. They will use arguments such as, "It's just a snow job. No one will offer you a referee who is going to say anything bad." There is, of course, an element of truth in this. Nonetheless, there are some tips, tools, and techniques precision recruiters use that make reference checking very worthwhile.

When Interviewing the Candidate

It might be true that no one offers a referee that would say bad things about the candidate, so get into the habit of asking to speak to people who are not necessarily offered as referees. For example, previous managers, peers who they have worked closely with, team members, even customers and suppliers.

As a rule of thumb, the lower level the job, the earlier in the recruitment process you should ask for referees. This will quickly sort out who is serious about getting the job and who is not.

Unfortunately, the more senior the role you are trying to fill, the more difficult it is to get an accurate reference. Often at these levels, deals are done in order to make it look as though the person has left of their own volition when, in actual fact, their previous manager was unable or unwilling to fire them.

When you ask the candidate for a referee, notice how quickly they are able to provide the names and numbers. It's not a foolproof method but the candidate who hesitates and has to think a bit might need a little more checking out than someone who has referees ready to go.

During the interview, ask the candidate to describe their previous manager's strengths and weaknesses. Also ask them to imagine what that manager would say the candidate's strengths and weaknesses are. Questions like these when also asked of the referee will provide you with some information that will quickly highlight consistencies and inconsistencies.

Speaking with the Referee

As well as asking the referee the questions we have just discussed, you would do well to consider asking:

- Questions related to the Key Selection Criteria
- "How would you advise me to manage this person?"
- "If there was one thing you could change about the candidate what would it be?"

and the old chestnut . . .

- "Would you hire them again?" or "Would you choose to work with them again?"

If you think that the referee is likely to speak very positively about the candidate, try beating them to it. Start off the conversation by stating what you already know about them that is good. This will increase the likelihood that the referee, in order to offer something of value, will talk about other things.

If they do start talking about something negative, your role is to stay silent. Do not finish their sentences for them. Do not even say "Hmm" or "U-huh," just let them go and listen very closely.

If you are a little hesitant to complete the reference check for whatever reason, there are professional organizations that offer reference checking and background checking services. Whether you do it yourself or pay someone else, you should ask yourself what could happen if you didn't reference check at all?

Other Reference Checks

Most people will beef up their resume by using words like "built" and "managed" when the truth is that they "had input to the design" and "assisted." This is what happens when we ask people to compete. There is a difference between beefing up a resume and lying.

It never ceases to amaze me the number of people who will out and out lie about what they have done. It may be necessary to do some additional checks to identify the truth behind some common areas where people may lie to get a job:

- university transcripts
- the Department of Immigration
- the Police

There are now organizations out there that focus on reference checking to a level that few middle managers are capable of. For more information, check out www.referencecheck.com.au

Other Forms of Assessment

Knowledge, Skill, and Attitude

Knowledge is cheap, knowledge is easy. Law of the markets states that any commodity of which there is a high volume will have a low value. You can hop on the Internet and download information, which is essentially knowledge, about anything you care to imagine. There are many smart people in this world and there are few successful people; however, you care to define success, because knowledge is not sufficient.

Let's say that we went to lunch and the service that we received was terrible. If we went to the person who served us at the end of the meal and asked them if they *knew* what it takes to provide good customer service, chances are that they would be able to tell us. Most people *know* how to provide good service and yet they still don't provide it.

Knowledge is close to useless until it is used. Knowledge is little until it is practiced. How is it that Olympic swimmers get to be Olympic swimmers? Not by reading how to swim on the Internet. At some stage they got wet! Knowledge requires words, skill requires practice.

And that's not all. Let's say that we complained to the manager of the person who gave us poor service at lunch. The manager then tells their team members to smile at the customers. Smiling is a *skill*, a micro-skill, but a skill nonetheless. The team member agrees to smile. Have you ever seen someone force a smile? Are you able to tell that it is a forced smile? Of course you can. Why? Because there is another aspect to top-quality performance . . .

And that's *Attitude*—your intention as you use the skill. Are you doing it because you have to or because you honestly believe that by using this skill it will make your job easier, produce better results, and increase others' respect for you?

The fact is that for top-quality performance you need all three. Knowledge, skill, and attitude. So when recruiting you are, no doubt, looking for a top-quality performer.

Poor recruiters will rely on questions that identify a candidate's knowledge only and make a decision on the candidate's responses to those questions. Then the interviewer wonders why they have hired a total jerk with low skill and a negative attitude. This is why, unless you are exceptionally skilled in the art of asking questions and listening to answers, it is wise to use some other forms of assessment.

Testing

Broadly speaking, testing can help identify a candidate's:

- Ability to perform or carry out different tasks (aptitude/skill),
- Motivation, values, and opinions around carrying out different tasks (interest/attitude),
- Style or manner of doing things, and in the way they interact with their environment and other people (personality/attitude).

The key here is not necessarily to use a popular test, although that has obvious merit, but rather to know what you are looking for and to know which test will best identify that.

As with reference checking, it would be unwise to use assessment centers and testing as a red or green light. The aim is to use a variety of methods, resumes, interviews, reference checks, and testing, and notice the patterns of behaviors that all of these tools highlight.

Assessment Centers

In recent years, a growing number of organizations have been using assessment centers as a recruitment tool. These centers, which comprise activities, exercises, or simulations, are designed to reflect common situations in the workplace. The recruiters observe the candidate's performance and make decisions, dependent on the result, about how the candidate's knowledge, skill, and attitude will fit into the role.

Assessment centers are typically used for high-volume, lower-level recruitment in areas such as call centers, and for maintenance staff and entry level positions.

The benefit of assessment centers, as with testing, is that they are another way of checking knowledge and skill on top of the recruitment interview. The challenge here is also to ensure that we are seeing the real person rather than the candidate showing their best side because they are going for a job. As such, assessment centers are rarely a good indicator of the attitude of the candidate.

Other Contexts

A colleague I once worked with would often take short-listed candidates out of the office for coffee or even lunch. He would say you could learn a lot about what it might be like to work with someone by the way they deal with other people when they feel as though they are not being watched. He would observe them talking to the people serving them in cafés and restaurants and notice their facial expressions, their tone of voice, their gestures, and so on. He would tell you that often a candidate has been a "Dr. Jekyll and Mr. Hyde" type, that is Dr. Jekyll when talking to him and Mr. Hyde when talking to the people serving them.

More Than One Perspective

We often refer to people who only have one way of looking at something as having tunnel vision. On top of this, when there is only two ways of looking at something, we call this a dichotomy. Dichotomies often leave us with the belief that one way is right and the other way is wrong. Wise people often seem to have the knack of looking at the same information from at least three different perspectives. This can provide added depth.

When it comes to recruitment, it would be unwise to hire someone based on one assessment method only. Having at least three different assessment methods provides us with a perspective that could not be achieved by interviewing only. Multiple perspectives can be gained through:

- More than one interview
- More than one interviewer
- Asking the candidates peers to interview
- Meeting the candidate over lunch
- Reference checking
- Profiling and testing
- Completing work samples
- Listening between the lines.

How to Handle Rejection

So let's say you have made your decision. You are as sure as you can be that you have the right person for the right job. You have offered them the position, they are ecstatic and they have accepted the position. Now all you need to do is phone up the other candidates and let them know that they were unsuccessful. Easy, right?

Easy if you are prepared to answer questions like:

- Could you please tell me why I was unsuccessful?
- Can you tell me why you chose the person you did over me?
- What feedback can you give me as I continue looking for a similar position?
- Are you sure you made the right decision?

When you are at the stage in the recruitment process of calling candidates up to let them know they were unsuccessful, you would know them pretty well by now. You would have interviewed them a couple of times, checked some references, and perhaps completed some other forms of assessment. You would know them well enough to be able to offer some constructive feedback.

There is a useful method that will help you do this. Use the EDI system (affectionately known as "Eddy") to help keep your feedback constructive, supportive, and balanced.

Effective

What did the person do that was really effective? What worked in their favor? What got them to a particular the stage in the recruitment process that they did? Please be as specific as possible . . . people love to know exactly what they did well!

Do More Of

What did the person do, have, or what were they, that if they did, had, or were it even more or even bigger or just more often, it would really help them get a similar position next time around? Again be specific.

Improve

What would be your *positive* suggestions for improvement? How could they do it even better next time? Phrase your suggestions positively by outlining what they *should be* doing, not what they should *stop* doing.

Sometimes the feedback here could be that the person did not sell themselves well enough on a particular point.

Finally, conclude with some overall, global statements of appreciation that are linked back to what they did well. You don't need to be specific here, so feel free to be global and fluffy!

CHAPTER 9

How to Speed Up the Return on Your Investment

Induction and Orientation

A very good friend of mine is a highly successful business person. She has established a number of businesses from idea through product launch and beyond. I can remember attending the opening of one of her businesses: a healthy, vegetarian, fast food outlet. She had run a clever marketing campaign in the lead up to the opening and so the first day was a big day. The press were there, there was some fine-tuning to processes required, people were queued outside the door for most of the day, and customers were being as demanding as they tend to be when they are waiting.

Despite all this, the team behind the counter operated exceptionally well considering it was their first day with real customers. I can remember asking the business owner some questions to find out what had been done to help make the team operate so well on their first day. One of her answers has stuck with me ever since.

She said, "If anything goes wrong in the first six months of a team member's employment, it's my fault."

"How do you figure that?" I asked.

"Well, I find that most people in their first six months of work remain pretty enthusiastic about the job," she replied. "If you have recruited well, they want to do a good job. So the responsibility lies squarely with me to make sure they are able to do the job the way it needs to be done."

If only every manager thought and acted like this!

Carefully considering a professional approach to induction and orientation will go a long way to minimizing the period it takes for new team members to become productive.

You will find an example of an induction checklist in the Appendices at the end of the book. Listed here is a comprehensive, but by no means exhaustive, list of items you might need to cover with a new team member.

Organizational Level

- The organization's history, current position, and future direction
- The organization's Key Performance Indicators—what do you use to assess how well the organization is performing?
- Industry-specific information (e.g., specific legislation)
- Occupational health and safety issues
- The organization's key/topical policies
- The organization's structure
- Introduction to the management
- Employment benefits and conditions
- The organization's performance management system, training, and career development opportunities
- Some of the organization's jargon and common terms

Team/office

- Introductions to team members
- Access keys/cards and any login identification needed
- Business cards
- Telephone list and email details
- Office plan—stationery, fire exits, toilets, and so on
- Employment paperwork (e.g., employment declaration, payroll advice, union application forms)

Job Specific

- Introduction to their buddy
- Job description
- Tools (e.g., computer, intranet, machinery, and so on)

- Coaching in each component of their job using the following suggested format:

  - Why this needs to be done,
  - What the task is,
  - How to do it—the procedure,
  - What to look out for when completing the task.

What Happens after That?

A widely accepted rule of thumb is that on average a new employee should be performing at an acceptable level after around 6 months. This is, of course, dependent on many factors, such as the complexity of the job, the seniority of the role, the amount you are paying, and so on.

For very senior or very simple roles, people should be able to contribute more than they cost a little quicker than 6 months. It is a potential warning sign if people are still not performing to expectations before 9 months.

Recruiting well is not a guarantee of good performance. Team members will perform above and beyond expectations if they have:

- Clear direction
- Competence
- Commitment
- Resources.

If any one of these is missing, performance is likely to be below expectations. The leader's role is to monitor and manage these. How to do that is surely the topic of another book. It certainly is . . . and that book is called . . .

Practical Performance Improvement . . . with Impact

How to:

- Reduce the stress associated with leading a team of people
- Improve the likelihood that things get done right . . . first time
- Be an exceptional leader.

APPENDIX

Job Aids, Reference Documents, and Freebies

But wait, there's more . . .

How to Use the Tools in This Section

In this section, we have included a range of job aids, reference documents, and freebies to be copy, use, and change as you see fit:

- Job description
- Sample receipt of application letter or email
- A library of questions
- Legal and illegal questions
- A structured interview guide
- Interview checklist
- Letter to an unsuccessful candidate
- Reference check questionnaire
- Induction/Orientation checklist for managers.

If you use the tools in this section, all we ask is that, as with any other part of this book that you use, you acknowledge where they came from on your copy of the form.

If you would like to save yourself a lot of typing, a soft copy of the appendices is available in either Microsoft Word or PDF format. Please contact us at Impact Human Performance Technologies and order out Precision Recruitment Skills Toolkit on CD.

Thank you in advance . . .

Job Description

Job Title: _____

Classification: _____   Date prepared: _____

Location: _____

Immediate Supervisor: _____

Job Summary _____

Nature & Scope _____

• Operating environment
• Reporting relationships
• Major responsibilities
• Key contacts
• Constraints
• Challenges

Position Dimensions

Subordinates:

Operating Budget:

Others

Key Accountabilities & Key Performance Indicators

Selection Criteria

   Essential
   Desirable

SAMPLE RECEIPT OF APPLICATION LETTER
OR EMAIL

Date

John Smith
25 Victoria Avenue
Crows Nest NSW 2065

Dear Mr. Smith

Thank you for applying for the position of   at   .
We plan to hold interviews for this position within three weeks
after the closing date for applications. If you are successful
in being short listed for interview, we will be in contact by
telephone to arrange a suitable interview date and time.

If you have not been contacted within this period, you can
assume that you have not been successful with your application
at this time.

Sincerely,

A Library of Interview Questions

Contents

Achievement Orientation
Adaptability
Assertiveness
Communication Skills
Creativity
Customer Service
Delegating
Initiative and Drive
Interpersonal Skills and Sensitivity
Managing People and Building a Team
Motivation
People Orientation
Persuading and Influencing
Problem Solving and Planning
Resilience
Tenacity
Strengths, Limitations and Training Needs
Teamwork
Work Ethic

Achievement Orientation

Q1. What matters most to you in your work?
Q2. Can you think of a situation where you consciously set a goal and achieved it?
   a) Please describe the situation that led you to set the goal.
   b) What did you do specifically to achieve the goal?
   c) How did it turn out?
Q3. What would you most like to achieve but have been unable to? Why were you unable to achieve it?
Q4. What goals have you presently set for yourself in different areas of your life?

Q5. What would make you suitable for this job?

Q6. What makes your day and what ruins your day?

Adaptability

Q1. What are the biggest changes you have been part of and how did you cope?

Q2. Describe the challenges that have really tested your adaptability.

Q3. Describe how you have initiated change. What was the outcome? What would you do differently next time?

Q4. What was the most significant thing you learned from implementing these changes?

Q5. What would you change in your current role if you had a free hand? Describe how you would go about it.

Q6. Who would you prefer to work with someone who was persistent or someone who was flexible? Why is that?

Assertiveness

Q1. Tell me about a time when one of your staff or a co-worker was not pulling their weight in the team.
What did you do? What was the result?

Q2. Describe how you have handled working as part of a committee or on a team-based project.

Q3. When you have worked on a project with others, how have you handled the situation when differences have arisen about how to complete the task?

Communication Skills

Q1. How would you describe your own communication style?

Q2. How do you ensure that your message is understood?

Q3. What sort of written communications have you prepared in the past?

Q4. Where could communication in your company be improved? What have you done to address that issue?

Creativity

Q1. What are the two projects you are proudest of completing.

Q2. Describe a problem for which your first solution did not work, so that you were forced to try other solutions.

a) How did this happen?

b) What did you do?

c) What was the result?

Q3. How do you help other people solve their work problems?

Customer Service

Q1. What do you think are the key elements of good customer service?

Q2. Can you describe for me a situation where you had to provide outstanding customer service?

a) What was the situation that led up to the incident?

b) What did you see as being required?

c) What action did you take?

Q3. Describe the most difficult customer you have had to handle. What did you do?

Delegating

Q1. What steps do you take to ensure that your department produces quality work?

Q2. How do you measure quality?

Q3. What method do you use to ensure that work gets done correctly and on time?

Q4. How do you make sure that your staff provide good service to other departments or customers?

Q5. Describe an employee who was very difficult to manage. How did you handle it?

Q6. What do you take into account when you have to plan and complete a project?

Initiative and Drive

Q1. Can you think of an example of a time you initiated a significant change in your company?
    a) What did you believe needed to happen?
    b) What did you do to implement the change?
    c) What was the final outcome?
Q2. What really challenges you?
Q3. What strategies/tactics do you use when you have a lot of work to do and only a little time to do it in?

Interpersonal Skills and Sensitivity

Q1. Have you changed your language to suit a particular audience? Describe the outcomes.
Q2. How do people around you differ in their "needs"? Give specific examples.
Q3. How do you let people know that you are listening and understanding them? Describe a specific incident.
Q4. Giving people feedback is often a test of our interpersonal skills. Tell me about the last time you had to give someone some bad news or negative feedback. What was the outcome?
Q5. Describe a situation you have been in where you were required to use some high-level interpersonal skills and show sensitivity.
    a) What did you believe would be the best way to handle this situation?
    b) What exactly did you do?
    c) What was the result of that action?
Q6. What type of people do you prefer to work with? What type of people do you not prefer to work with?

Managing People and Building a Team

Q1. Describe how you have developed staff in the past.
Q2. Describe what you have done to build high-performing teams.
Q3. How does your management style differ from your colleagues'? Is it successful? Give examples.

Q4. What are the biggest "people" problems you have faced and how did you overcome them?

Give a specific example.

Q5. Describe the most difficult person you have had to work with or for. What did you do to continue working with them?

Q6. No two employees are exactly alike. How do you take this into account when you manage them? Can you give me a specific example?

Q7. How do you set direction for your team?

Motivation

Q1. What things do you like best about your current job?

Q2. Describe a time when you worked particularly hard and felt a strong sense of achievement:

a) What was the situation that led up to the incident?

b) What exactly did you do?

c) Why did you feel you had achieved?

Q3. Describe some recent responsibilities you have taken on. Why did you assume these responsibilities?

Q4. Can you give me an example of experiences you felt were dissatisfying?

Q5. What motivates you to put in your greatest effort?

Q6. Under what conditions do you find yourself holding back your efforts?

Q7. Describe your ideal job. What would you be doing more of and less of?

Q8. How do you know when you have done a great job?

People Orientation

Q1. Can you think of a situation where the output of your job required you to work closely with other people?

a) Please describe the situation and why working closely with others was critical.

b) What did you do?

c) What was the result?

Q2. When you first approach someone you must talk with, what do you tend to do?

Q3. How do you weigh the relative importance of handling feelings versus handling facts in your relationships at work?

Q4. What factors have contributed most to your success in dealing with different types of people in jobs?

Q5. What would you like to get out of this job if it was offered to you?

Persuading and Influencing

Q1. Describe a time when you failed to sell a proposal or viewpoint to other people. What happened?

Q2. Describe your most disappointing experience in trying to get management to agree to a proposal of yours. What would you do differently next time?

Q3. How do you get your ideas accepted if you aren't in a position of authority with others?

Q5. Think of a time when you needed your boss to change the way they handled something. What happened and how did you handle it?

Q6. Tell me about a time when two people disagreed with you about an important situation. What did you do?

Problem Solving and Planning

Q1. How do you approach solving problems? Give us some examples of some real-life scenarios you've had to fix.

Q2. What are the most complex plans you have developed?

Q3. How do you keep yourself on track?

Q4. How have you built flexibility into your plans?

Q5. How do you approach project management?

Q6. What targets must your department accomplish and how do you make sure these targets are reached?

Q7. What was the most difficult decision you had to make? Why did you make that decision? What were the results of the decision?

Resilience and Tenacity

Q1. Describe how you felt after you lost that important customer.

Q2. Describe some of your biggest disappointments. What did you do the next day?

Q3. Describe one of the main obstacles you had to overcome to get where you are today.

Q4. Can you describe some experiences where you felt that you gained something because you persisted for a long time?

Q5. Can you describe a situation where you tried your best but did not succeed?

Q6. What hurdles did you overcome to get as far as you have in your career?

Q7. How do you deal with other people when they don't meet agreed deadlines?

Strengths, Limitations, and Training Needs

Q1. What do you see as your strengths?

Q2. What new skills would you like to develop?

Q3. What do you see as the greatest challenge for you in this role?

Q4. What was the most useful criticism you ever received?

Q5. If your last boss was able to waive a magic wand over your head, what aspect of your performance would change?

Q6. If you had the opportunity to do the final 10 years of your career all over again, what would you do differently?

Teamwork

Q1. Tell me how you prefer to carry out projects. Give an example.

Q2. What's most important to you when you work with other people?

Q3. Tell me about your best experience when working as part of a team.

Q4. How do you work best with people?

Q5. Describe some projects you had to do but later wished you had not been involved with.

Q6. How would we know if you were stressed?

Work Ethic

Q1. What do you think distinguishes a good employee from an average employee?

Q2. What are the standards of success in your current job?

Q3. Have you missed deadlines, targets, budgets? What were the causes?

Q4. If we had to choose between a person who was highly intelligent and puts in an average effort and a person who was of average intelligence and yet had a high work ethic, who would you recommend we choose and why?

A Structured Interview Guide

Position _____   Interview Date _____

Candidate _____   Contact No _____

Panel member _____

Establish Rapport   *Build Trust*   *Build Credibility*

Be aware of EEO/Anti-Discrimination requirements

Career Overview:

(Identify motivation behind each job change, highlights, and disappointments)

What values have been important to you in both your work and personal life?

Motivations for Change: Aspirations and Ambitions

Why did you apply for this job—what attracted you?

What job and corporate culture did you enjoy most?

Problem Solving and Planning

What targets must your department meet and how do you make sure these are reached?

People Management

How does your management style differ from that of your colleagues'? Can you give us some examples of where it has been successful?

How do you like to be managed?

Customer Service

Can you describe a situation where you consider that you gave outstanding customer service?

Teamwork

What's most important to you when you work with other people?

Communication

How do you ensure your message is understood?

Has there been an occasion when you were required to communicate verbally with a group of people who were intellectually disabled or deaf or unable to understand English? How did you overcome this problem?

People Orientation

What factors have contributed most to your success in dealing with different types of people in jobs?

When you come to work each day, what's the one ingredient in your job that makes you feel enthusiastic?

Persuading and Influencing

Describe a time when you failed to sell a proposal or viewpoint to other people. What went wrong?

How do you get your ideas accepted if you aren't in a position of authority with others?

Motivation

Describe times when you worked particularly hard and felt a strong sense of achievement.

Give me an example of experiences you found dissatisfying.

Overall Comments:

Interview Checklist

The structured interview format has five main stages:

1. Preparation
2. Building rapport
3. Framing up the process
4. Questioning to identify knowledge, skills, and attitude
5. Summary and closing

Preparation

Preparing What to Say and Ask

- Review the organization's values, the Key Selection Criteria, and the individual's resume.
- Use the above to identify areas you will be able to build rapport, and determine knowledge, skills, and attitude.
- List three to five questions you can ask that will help the candidate feel comfortable and perform at their best.
- Refer to the section earlier in this Appendix, "A Library of Interview Questions," to list questions you will ask during the interview.
- Write down and practice a phrase that will let the candidate know how the interview will run.
- Study the candidate's application and work history, and assess the information present and missing.
- Prepare a list of specific questions to ask.
- Build an interview guide.

Preparing the Environment

To convey a professional impression to the candidate, consider the work areas that they will be brought into contact with in the interview process:

- the reception area.
- the interview office.
- the successful applicant's work area.

Building Rapport

- Be on time.
- When candidate arrives and is taken to interview room, make sure they are offered tea/coffee and so on and given time to relax.
- Introduction. State your role in the company. Notice their handshake, dress, overall first impression and so on.
- Note down your first impressions, record what you see and hear.

Framing Up the Process

Here's an example:

> *"Chris, the way we'd like to run the interview is:*
>
> *"Firstly, I'll give you a brief overview of the organization, the division in which the vacancy exists and a little about the position that we are looking to fill.*
>
> *"After that we will be asking you a few questions to find out as much as we can about you, your experience and expertise, and your suitability for the position.*
>
> *"Thirdly, if you have any questions you would like to ask us we will do our best to ensure you leave here with a crystal clear understanding of what it is like to work here.*
>
> *"And then finally we will summarize what we have covered and discuss what the next steps are.*
>
> *"All of this should take about an hour. How does that sound?"*

Questioning to Assess Knowledge, Skills, and Attitude

Ask the candidate to talk through their career to date, starting in the past and working forward. Ask the candidate to elaborate on career highlights and reasons for job changes, major projects, and so on. This "big long question" places the burden on the interviewee and saves you asking a large number of the same questions about each job. Note what is "glossed over," highlighted, and so on, and note patterns and anomalies. Follow these up.

Summary and Closing

- Identify the areas you thought the candidate was most strong in.
- Identify the areas you thought the candidate will find most challenging.
- Get the candidate's feedback and reaction.
- Advise the candidate about the specific organizational requirements for that position (e.g., dress, appearance, parking arrangements, employment status).
- Close the interview.
- Informal chat.
- Say goodbye.
- Evaluate the interview—compare information gained to selection criteria and rate the candidate.
- Decide on next steps, do not delay—good candidates rapidly go off the market.

SAMPLE LETTER OR EMAIL TO AN UNSUCCESSFUL CANDIDATE

Dear

Thank you for meeting with us to discuss the position of   . It was interesting discussing your background and experience in more detail.

Although you were among a number of high-caliber applicants we interviewed for this position, unfortunately you were not successful in obtaining this particular role.

Thank you for the interest you showed in joining our company. We would like to keep your resume on file, to consider you if another suitable role comes up in the near future.

Yours sincerely,

Sample Reference Check Questionnaire

Name of candidate   _____

Name of Referee   _____

Name of reference checker _____

Company/Department   _____

Date   _____

Alex has applied for a position as a Sound Operator and has given you as a referee.

Would you be willing to answer some questions relating to their previous employment with your company? Thank you.

What was their position in the company?

Over what period were they employed there?

What was their relationship to you in the company?

I'd just like to outline the main responsibility areas in this new role. Where do you see them making their major contribution to this role?

Where do you think they may have difficulties?

How would you describe their personality?

What is their communication style like?

How would the team that worked for them have described them?

How would their peers/superiors have described them?

What are they like working in a team?

How is their ability to achieve results?

What are their energy levels like? Are they motivated in their daily work?

How persuasive are they?

Are they a good (strategic) planner? Can they think through a plan's implications?

Can they make difficult decisions on people?

What are they like under pressure?

Where do you think is their greatest need for development?

How would you rate then in the role in which you employed them?

Would you hire them again?

_____   _____

Reference Check completed by   Date

Sample Induction/Orientation Checklist for Managers

Pre-arrival

- ❑ Employee Manual prepared:
    - ○ Business cards
    - ○ Telephone lists
    - ○ Office plan (i.e., who sits where, exits and so on)
    - ○ Organizational structure chart
- ❑ Information on the organization's vision, mission, and values
- ❑ Desk set up including stationery, telephone, and computer
- ❑ Access card/keys
- ❑ Logon id
- ❑ Systems access arranged for:
    - ○ Email
    - ○ Any specific programs
- ❑ Allocate "Buddy" from team if appropriate

First day

- ❑ Review Employee Manual with new employee
- ❑ Ensure that all appropriate paperwork is completed
- ❑ Introductions to main people in their area

Ensure appropriate forms are completed and returned

- ❑ Employment Declaration (tax form)
- ❑ Payroll Advice Form
- ❑ Application to Superannuation Fund
- ❑ Signed letter of appointment
- ❑ Union application form
- ❑ Social Club application form

Within a month of commencement

- ❑ Induction evaluation completed and returned
- ❑ Completion of Employee Development Plan

About the Author

Rod Matthews has an international reputation as a leading authority on change and human performance and has unashamedly been described as "the best trainer in Australia." He is skillfully able to engage groups of people and move them from a place of confusion and sometimes even hostility to a place of confidence, clarity, and consensus. Rod delivers on his promise and "gets the message across" by engaging his audience with wit and intelligence and with entertaining, dynamic, and practical training methodologies. Rod works for all organizations across all industries—wherever there are people. For over 20 years, his experience, enthusiasm, and natural curiosity have allowed him to build an encyclopedic knowledge of tips, tools, and techniques that inspire, motivate, inform, and educate. Rod's qualifications include: Graduate Certificate of Study Integrated Human Studies—University of Western Australia; Certificate of Leadership—Cornell University; Certificate of Qualification of Educational Applications of Generative Learning and Neuro-Linguistic Programming; and Graduate Diploma of Adult Education. His accreditations include: The Leadership Circle, Myers–Briggs Type Indicator, and DiSC Profile.

Index

OTHER TITLES IN THE HUMAN RESOURCE MANAGEMENT AND ORGANIZATIONAL BEHAVIOR COLLECTION

- *Practical Performance Improvement: How to Be an Exceptional People Manager* by Rod Matthews
- *Creating Leadership: How to Change Hippos Into Gazelles* by Philip Goodwin and Tony Page
- *Uncovering the Psychology of Good Bosses vs Bad Bosses and What it Means for Leaders: How to Avoid the High Cost of Bad Leadership* by Debra Dupree
- *Competency Based Education: How to Prepare College Graduates for the World of Work* by Nina Morel and Bruce Griffiths
- *Phenomenology and Its Application in Business* by Roger Sages and Abhishek Goel
- *Organizational Design in Business: A New Alternative for a Complex World* by Carrie Foster
- *The 360 Degree CEO: Generating Profits While Leading and Living with Passion and Principles* by Lorraine A. Moore
- *Power Quotes: For Life, Business, and Leadership* by Danai Krokou
- *Magnificent Leadership: Transform Uncertainty, Transcend Circumstance, Claim the Future* by Sarah Levitt
- *Negotiating with Winning Words: Dialogue and Skills to Help You Come Out Ahead in Any Business Negotiation* by Michael Schatzki
- *Conflict First Aid: How to Stop Personality Clashes and Disputes from Damaging You or Your Organization* by Nancy Radford
- *Temperatism, Volume I: A New Way to Think About Business and Doing Good* by Carrie Foster
- *The Challenge to Be and Not to Do: How to Manage Your Career and Maximize Your Potential* by Carrie Foster
- *Slow Down to Speed Up: Lead, Succeed, and Thrive in a 24/7 World* by Liz Bywater

Announcing the Business Expert Press Digital Library

Concise e-books business students need for classroom and research

This book can also be purchased in an e-book collection by your library as

- *a one-time purchase,*
- *that is owned forever,*
- *allows for simultaneous readers,*
- *has no restrictions on printing, and*
- *can be downloaded as PDFs from within the library community.*

Our digital library collections are a great solution to beat the rising cost of textbooks. E-books can be loaded into their course management systems or onto students' e-book readers.
The **Business Expert Press** digital libraries are very affordable, with no obligation to buy in future years. For more information, please visit **www.businessexpertpress.com/librarians**. To set up a trial in the United States, please email **sales@businessexpertpress.com**.

www.ingramcontent.com/pod-product-compliance
Lightning Source LLC
Chambersburg PA
CBHW071910200326
41519CB00016B/4552